Adult Coloring Book

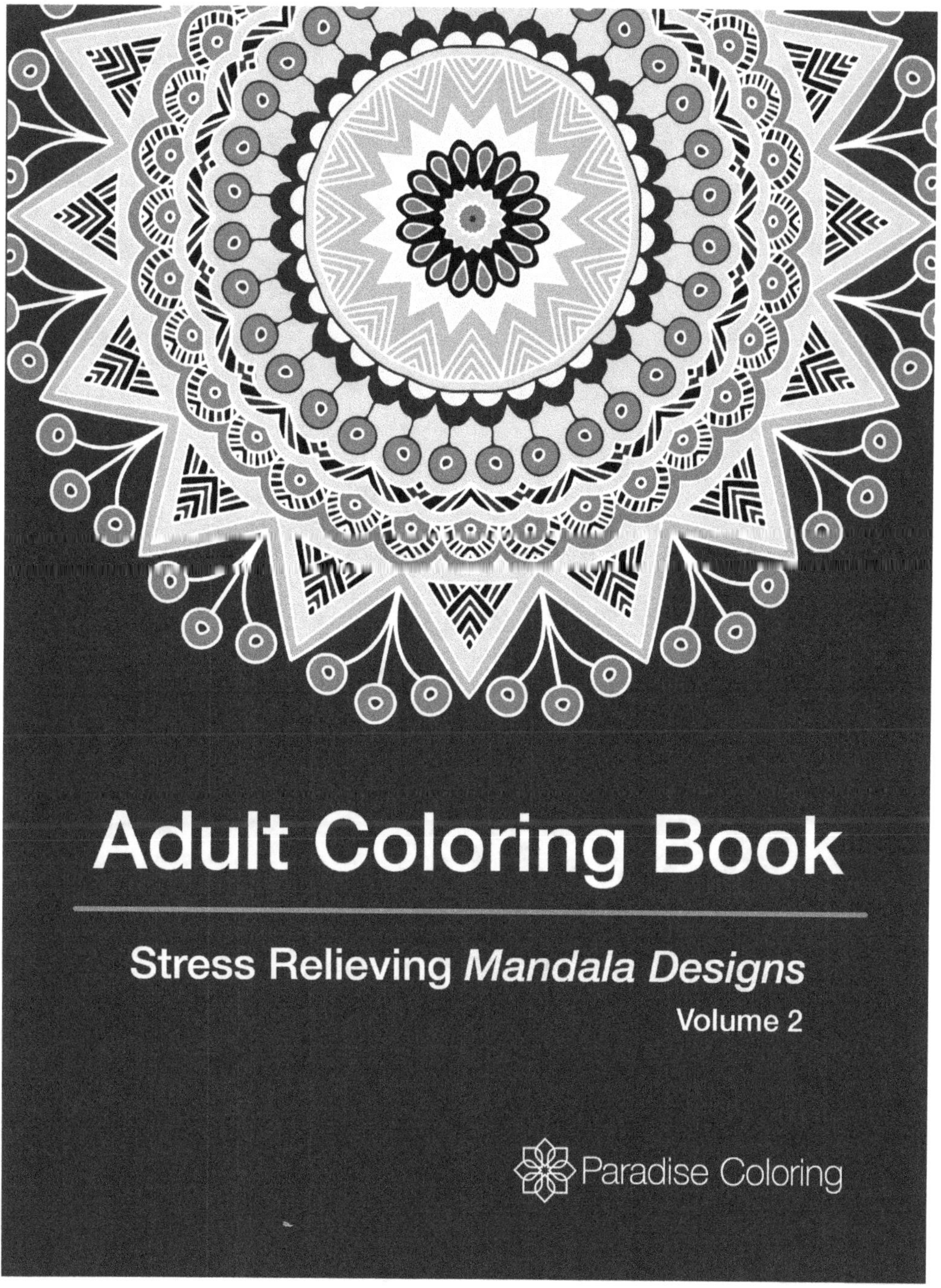

Stress Relieving *Mandala Designs*

Volume 2

Paradise Coloring

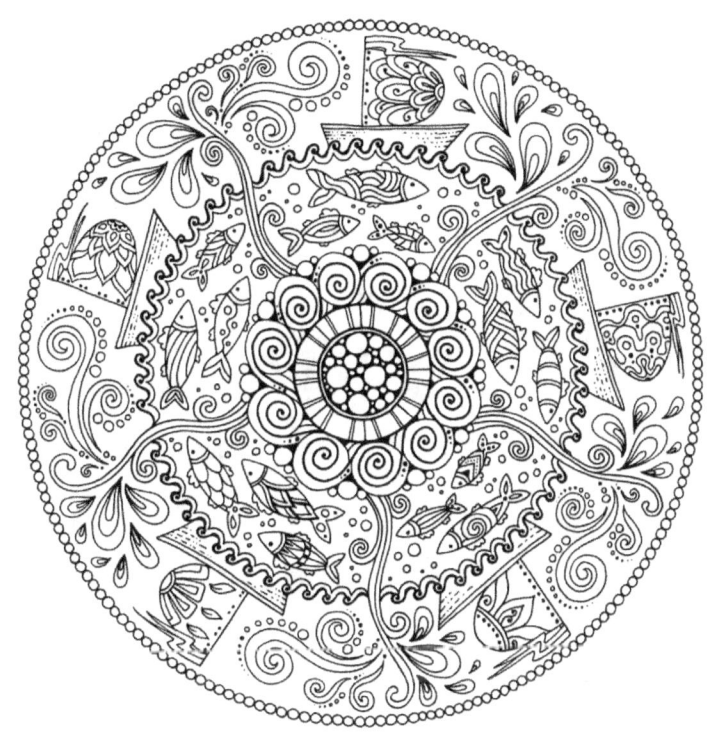

This book belongs to:

_____

I can't change the direction of the wind, but I can adjust my sails to always reach my destination.

-Jimmy Dean

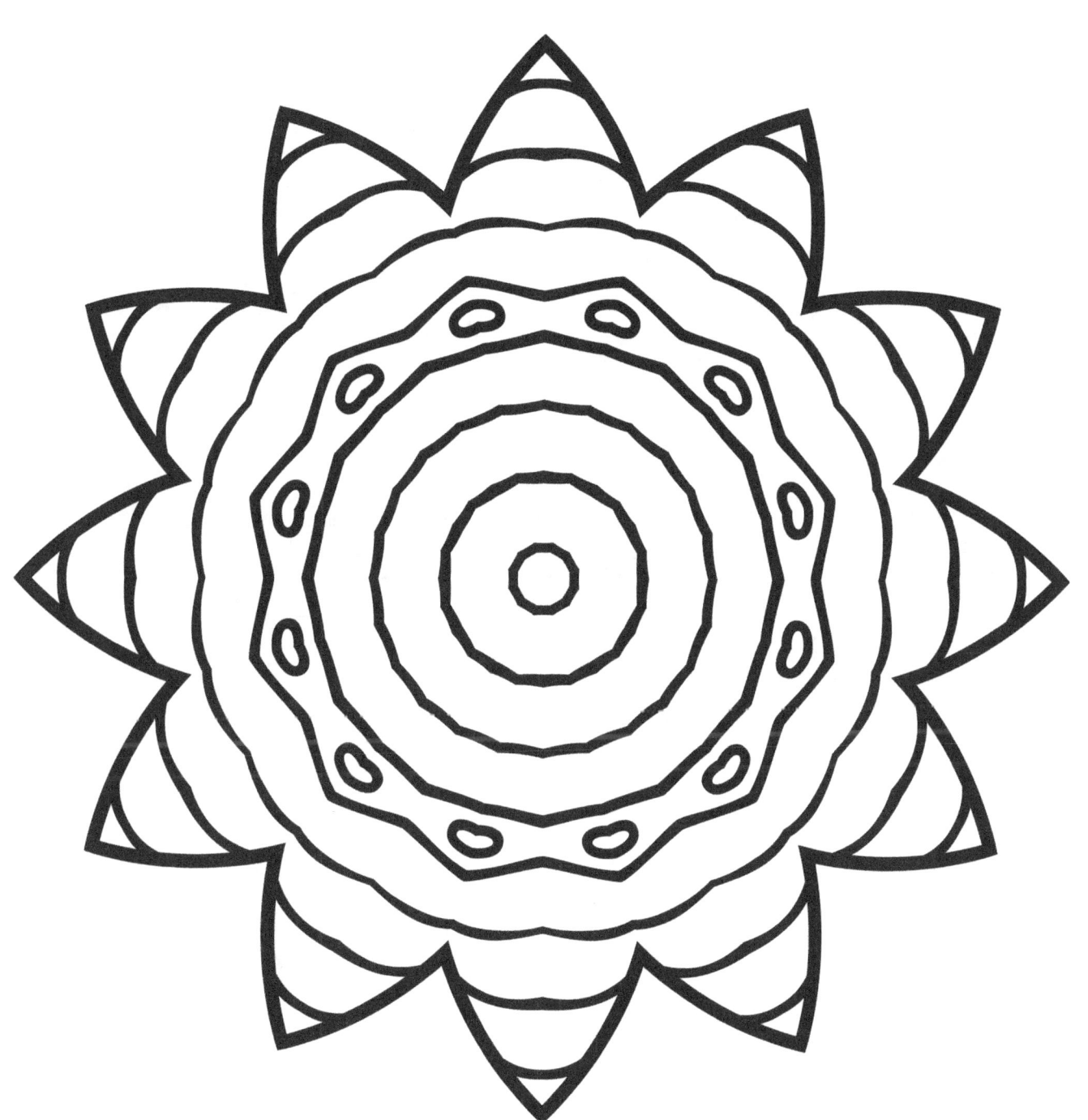

Believe you can and you're halfway there.
                    -Theodore Roosevelt

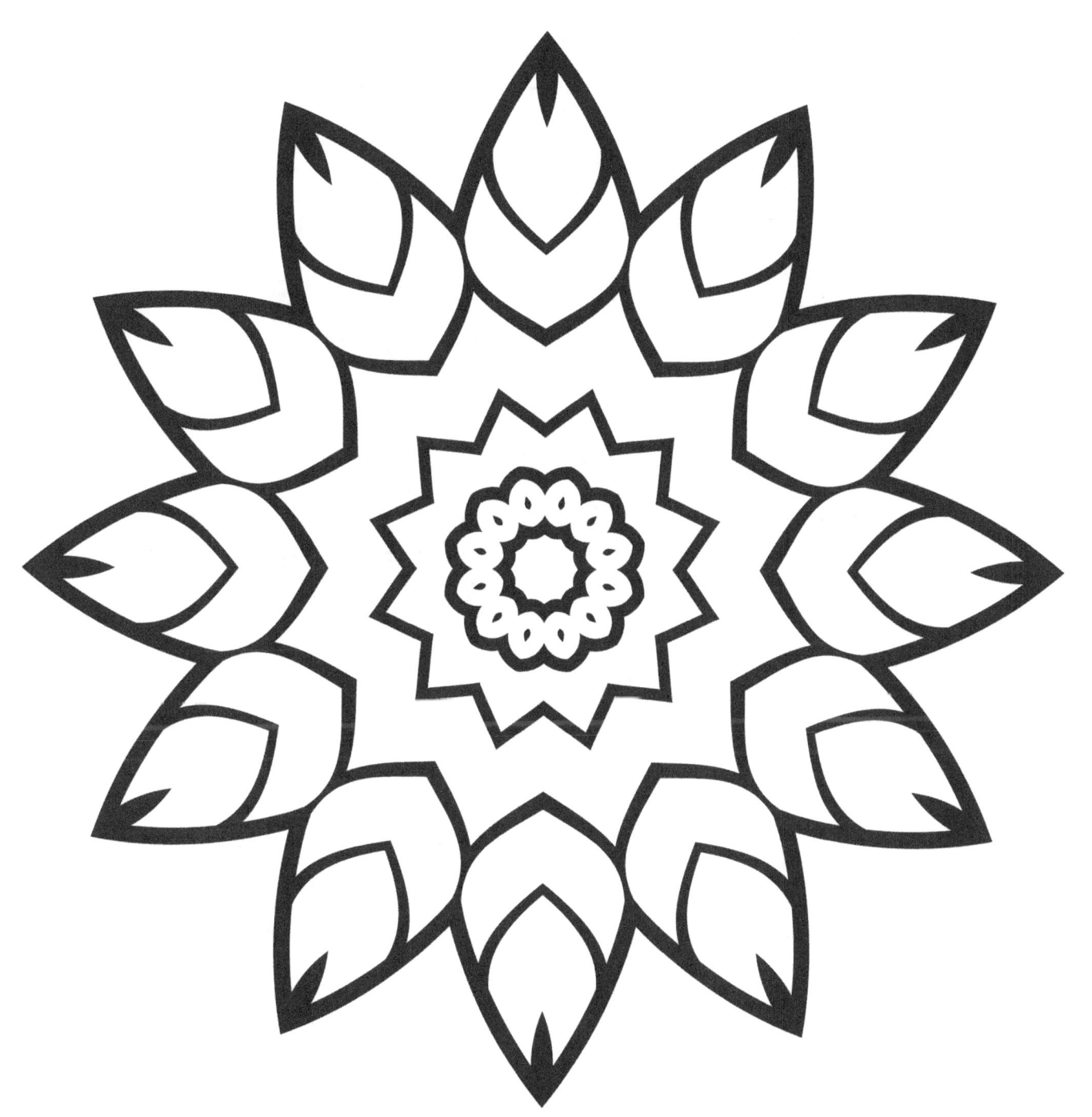

The measure of who we are is what we do
with what we have.

-Vince Lombardi

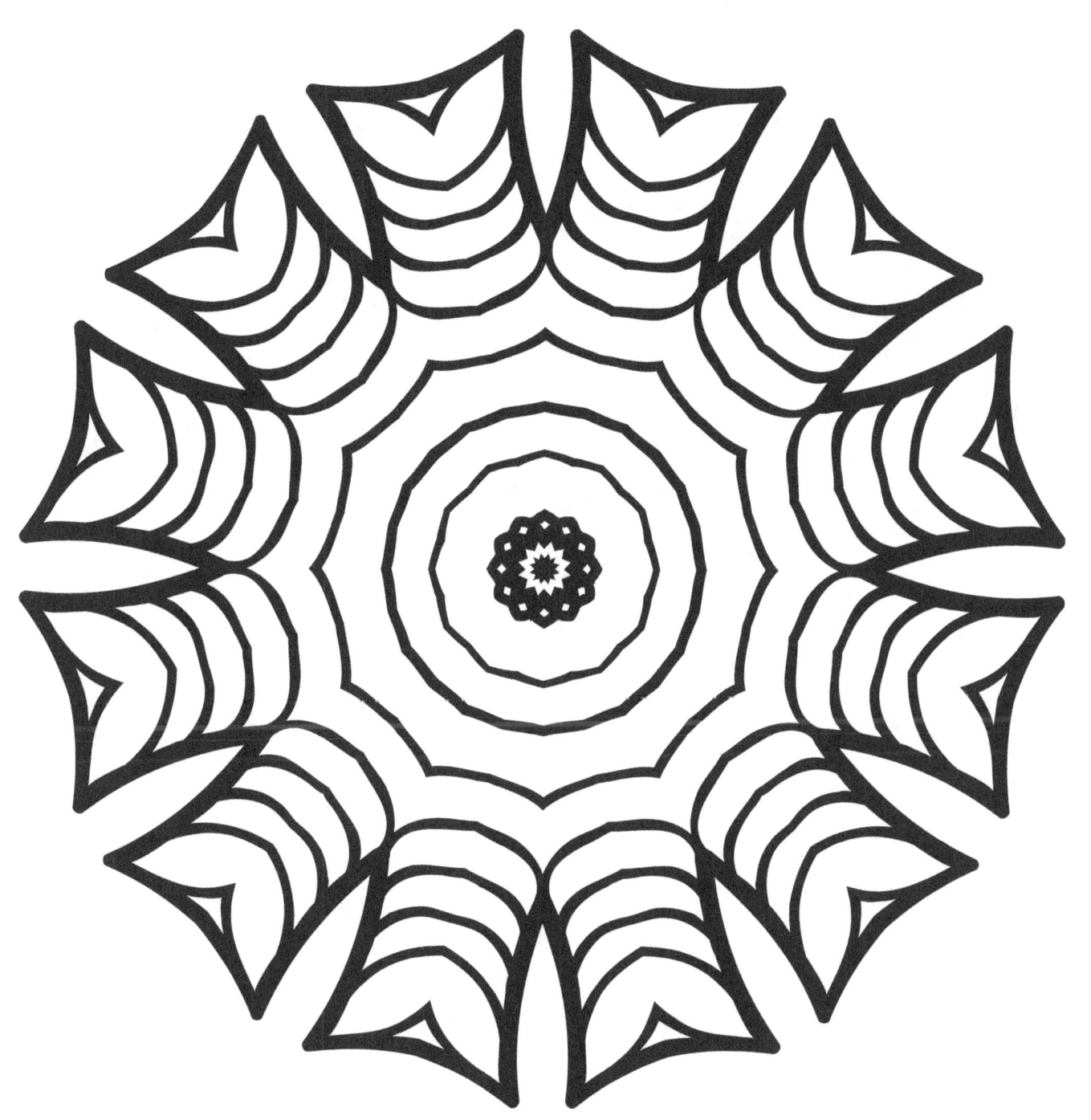

I hated every minute of training, but I said,
'Don't quit'. Suffer now and live the rest
of your life as a champion.

-Muhammad Ali

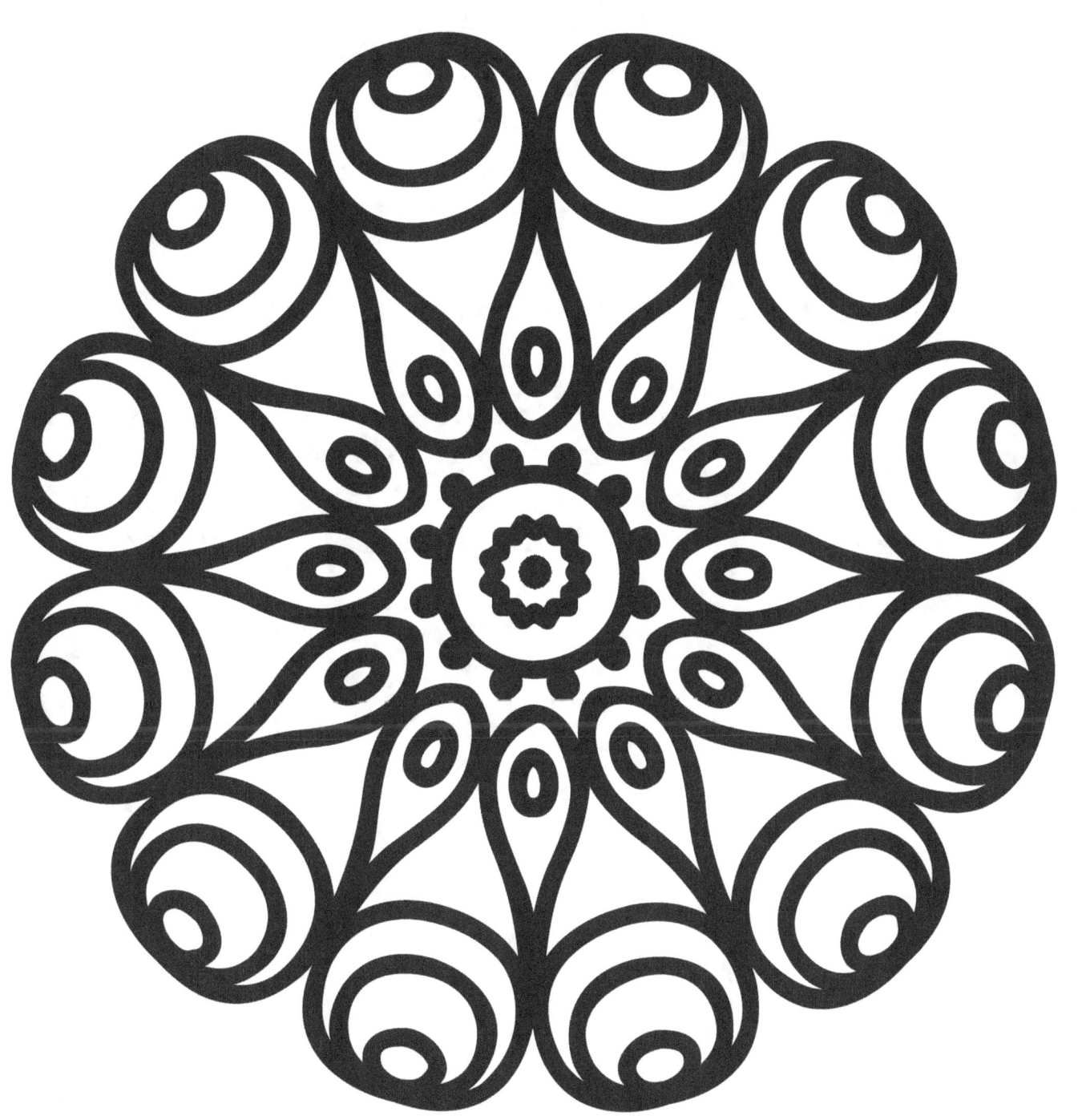

Whoever is happy will make others happy too.

-Anne Frank

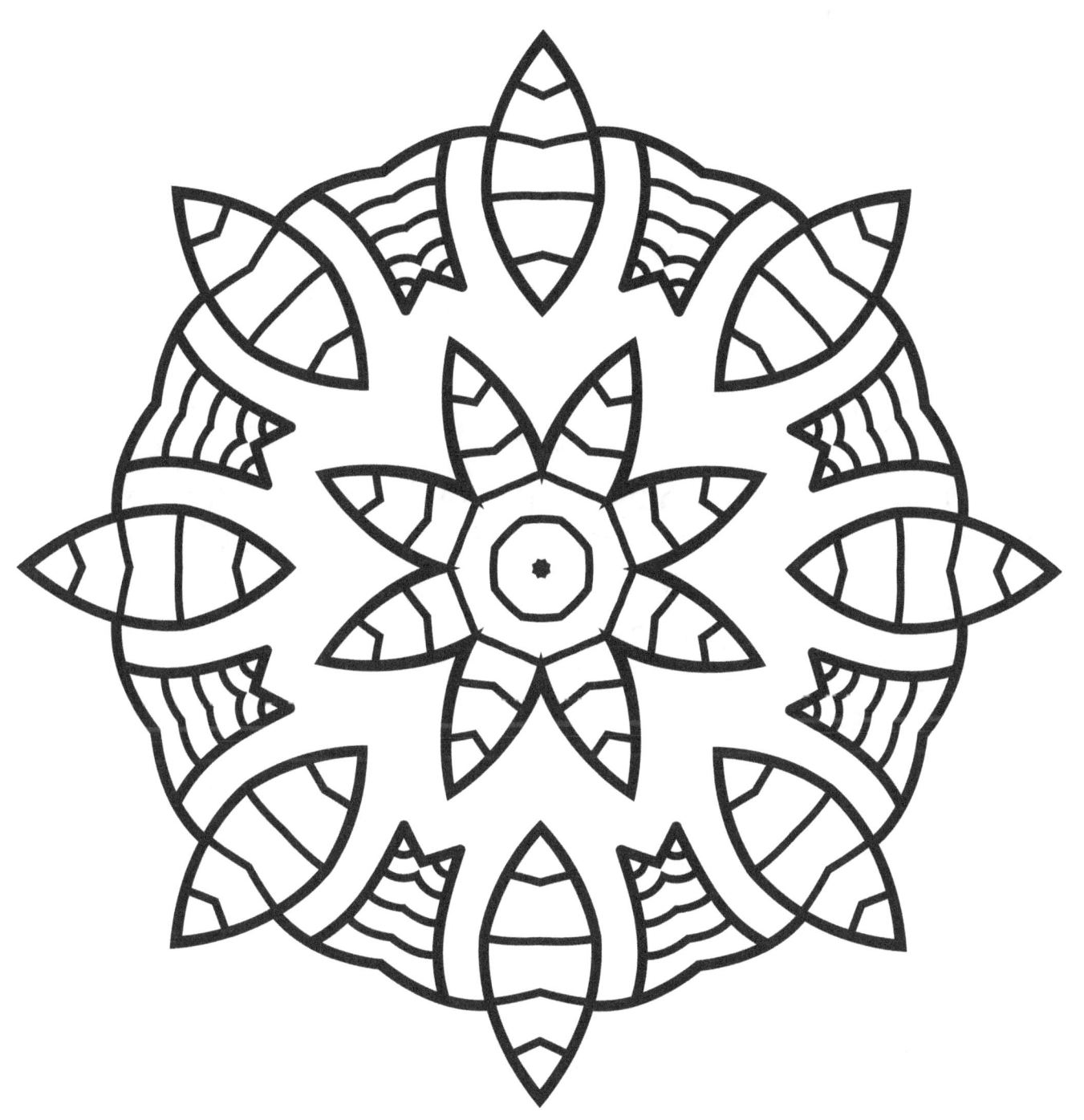

Clouds come floating into my life, no longer to carry rain or usher storm, but to add color to my sunset sky.

-Rabindranath Tagore

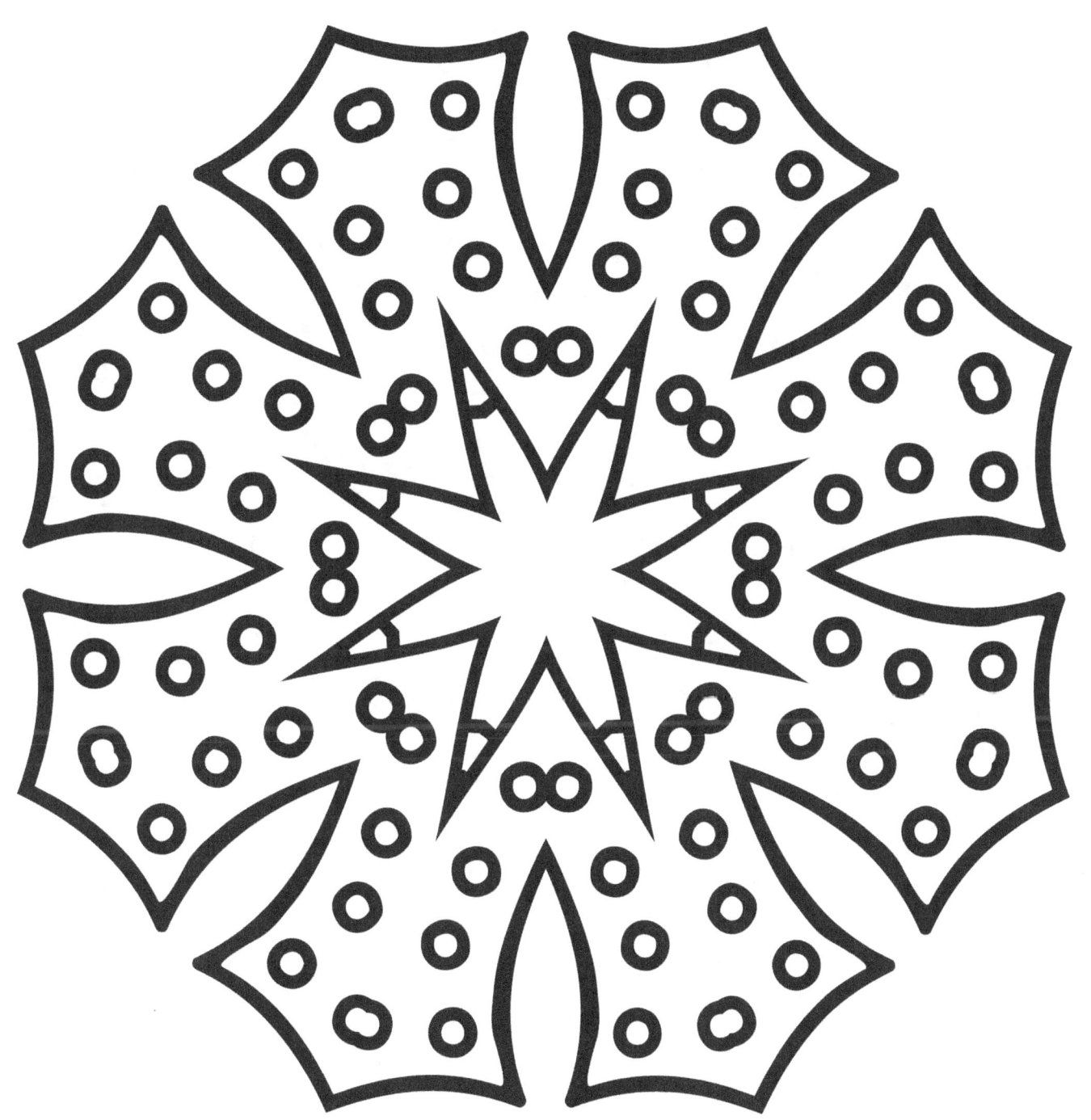

Keep your face always toward the sunshine
and shadows will fall behind you.

-Walt Whitman

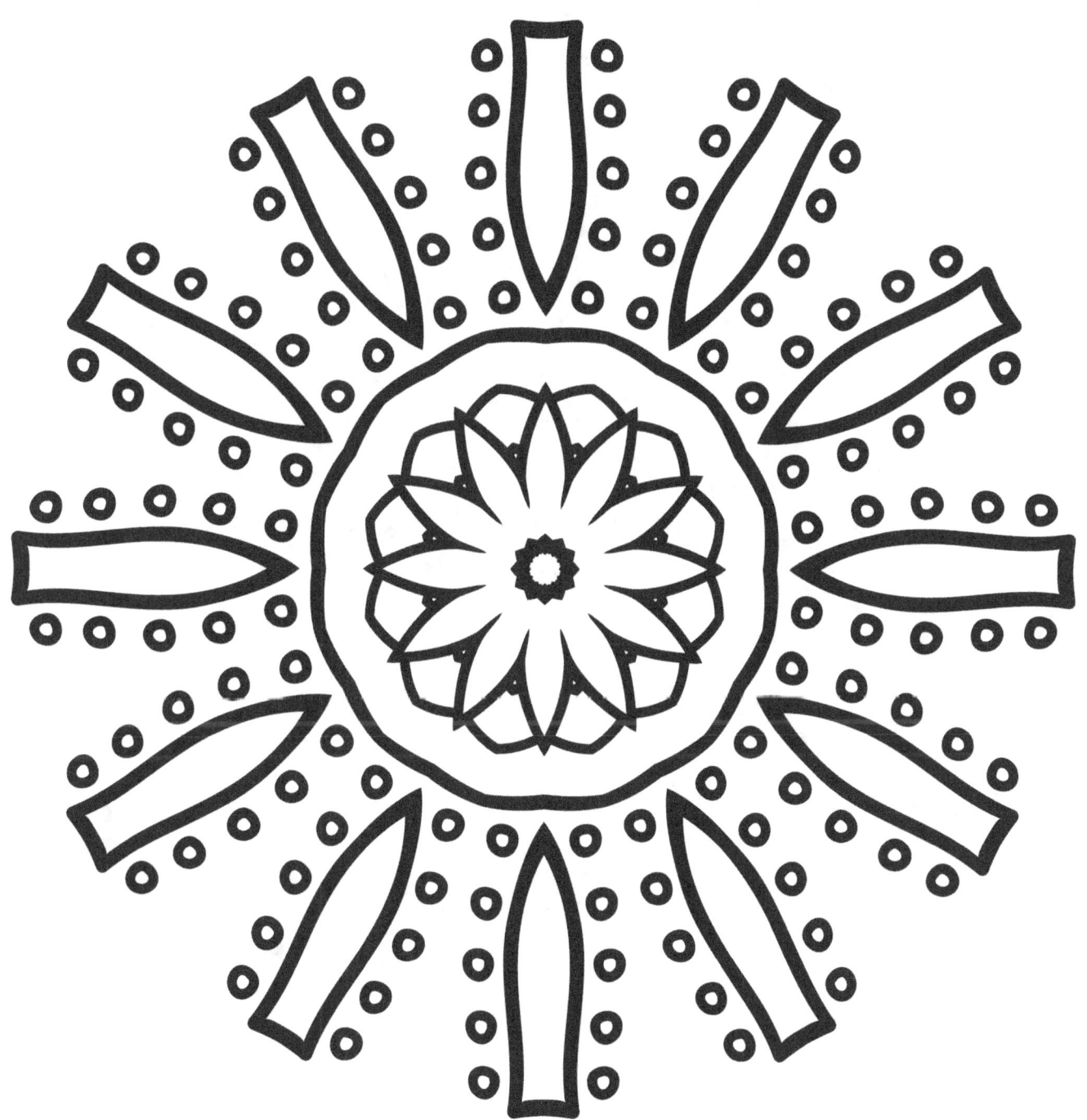

It is in your moments of decision that
your destiny is shaped.

-Tony Robbins

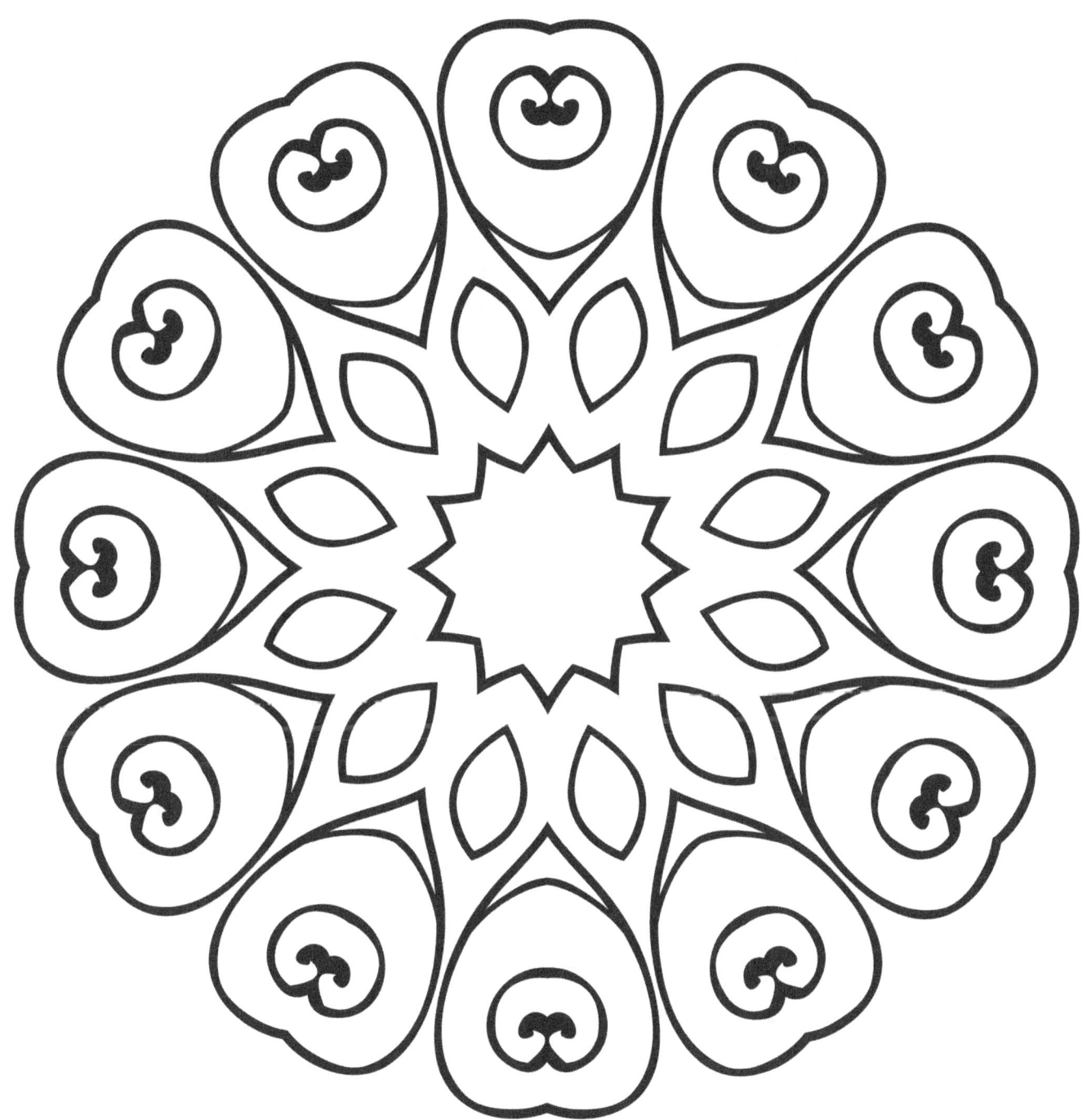

What lies behind you and what lies in front of you,
pales in comparison to what lies inside of you.

-Ralph Waldo Emerson

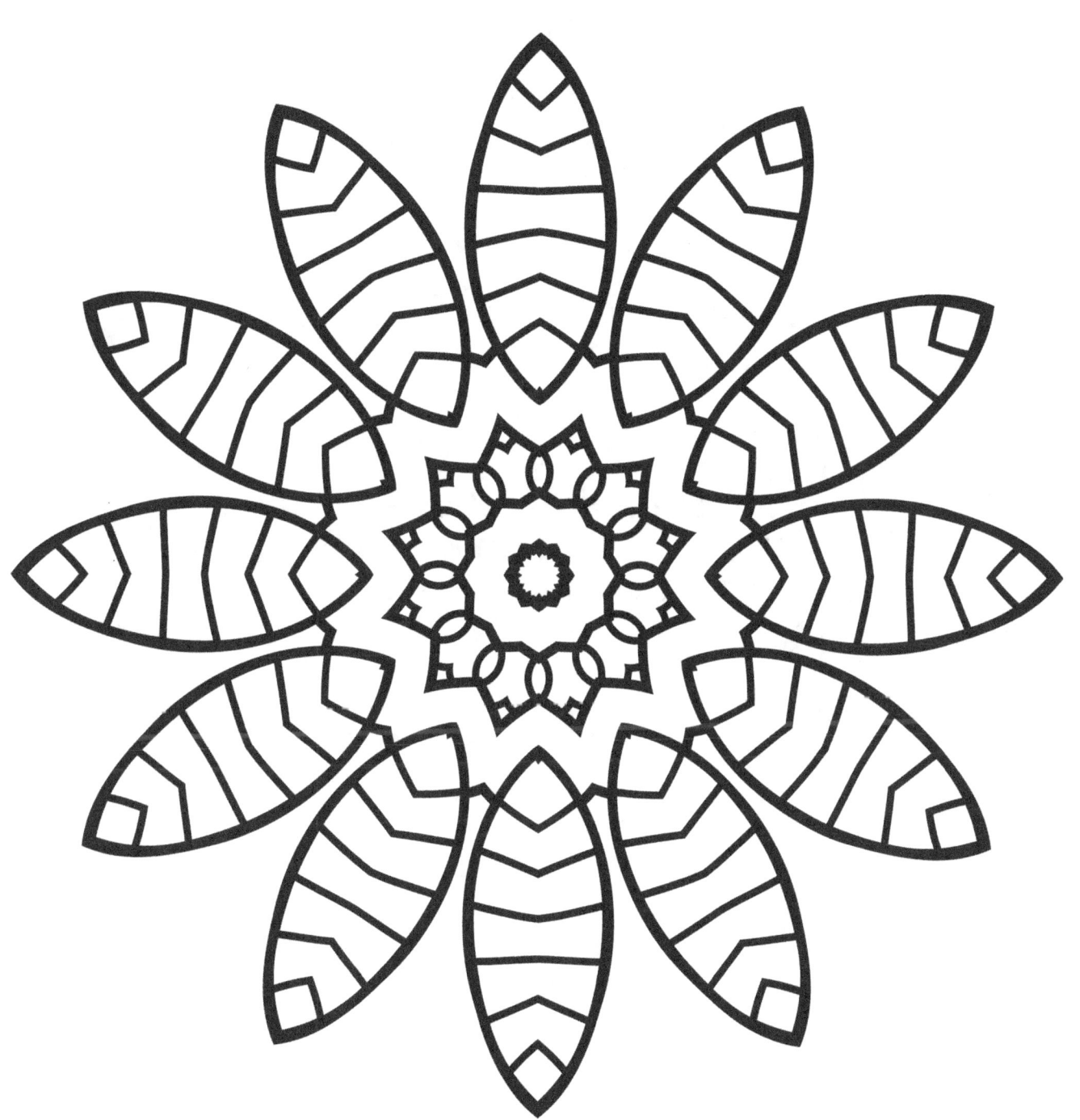

I will love the light for it shows me the way,
yet I will endure the darkness because
it shows me the stars.

-Og Mandino

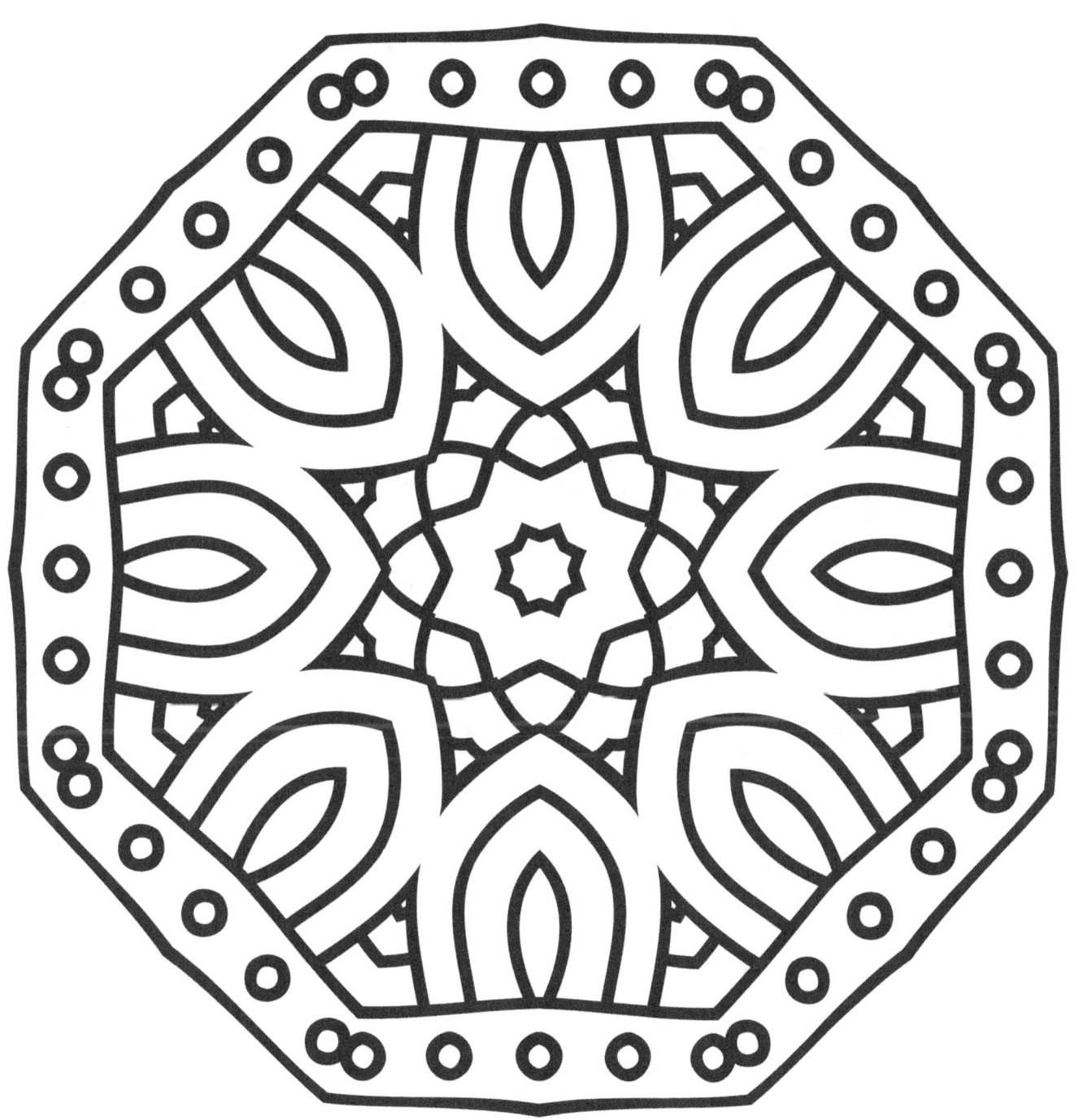

Holding on to anger is like grasping a hot coal with
the intent of throwing it at someone else;
you are the one who gets burned.

– Buddha

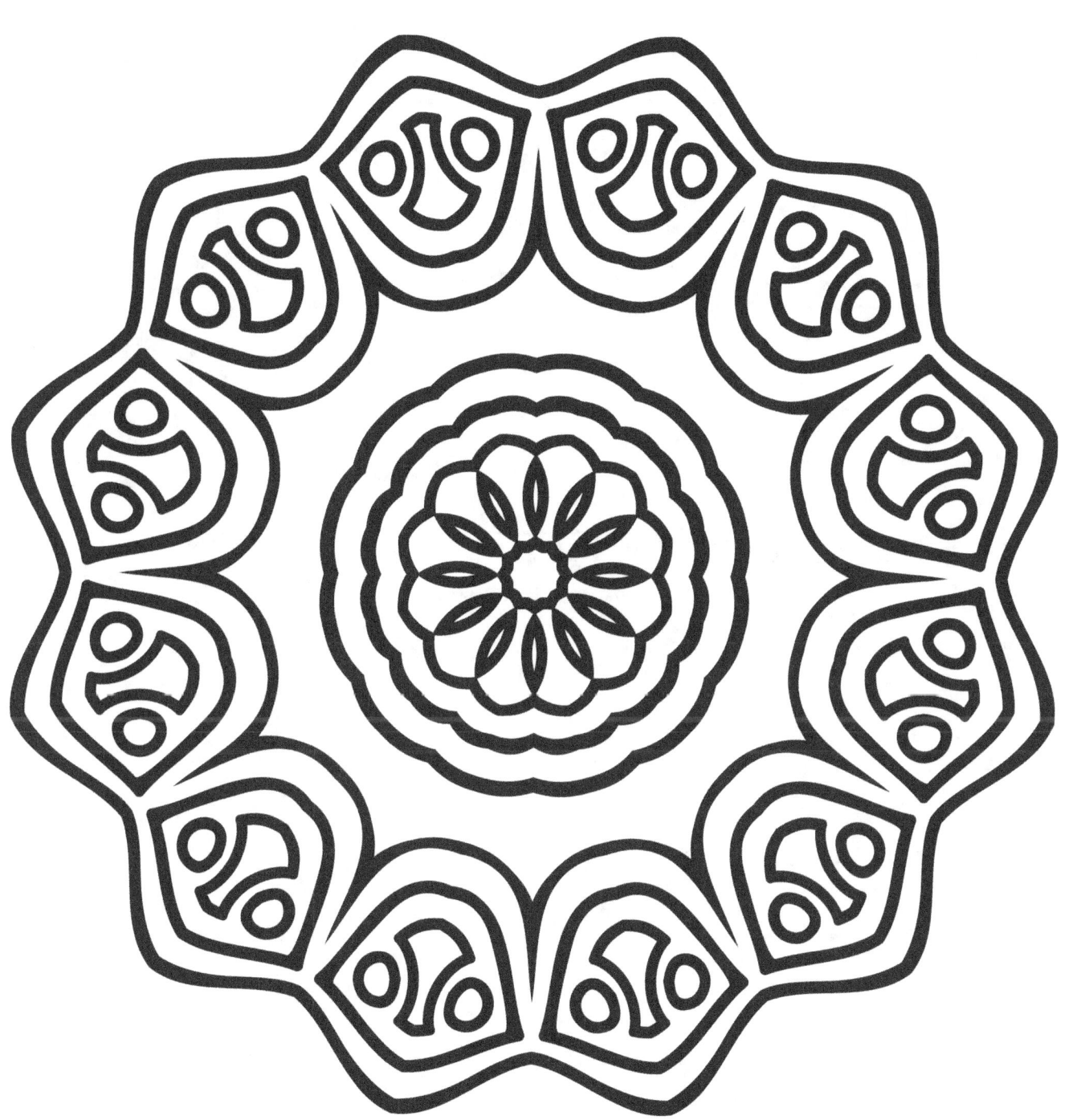

"STRESSED" is "DESSERTS" spelled backwards.

-Author Unknown

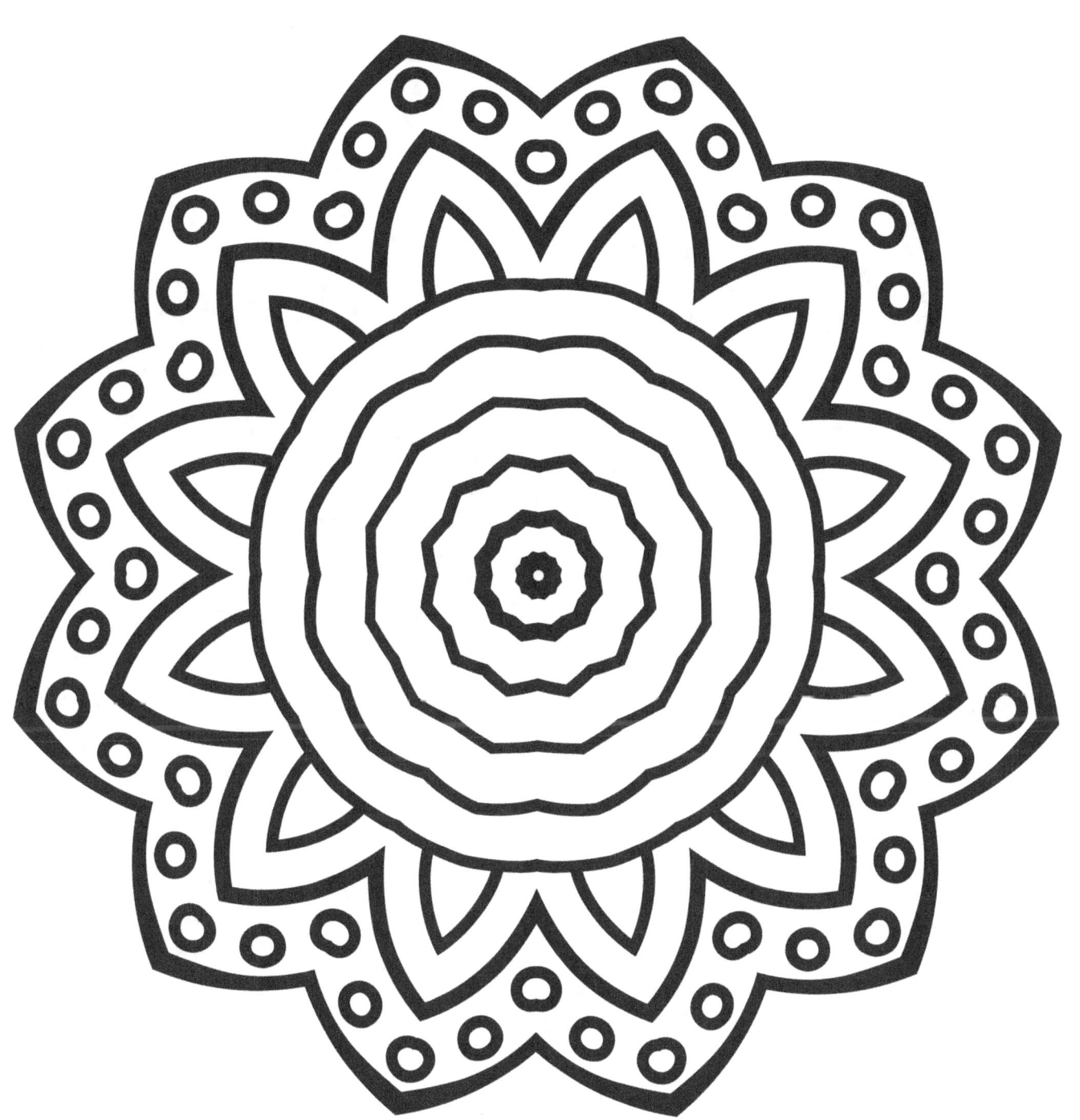

The best preparation for tomorrow is
doing your best today.

-H. Jackson Brown, Jr.

Out of difficulties grow miracles.

-Jean de la Bruyere

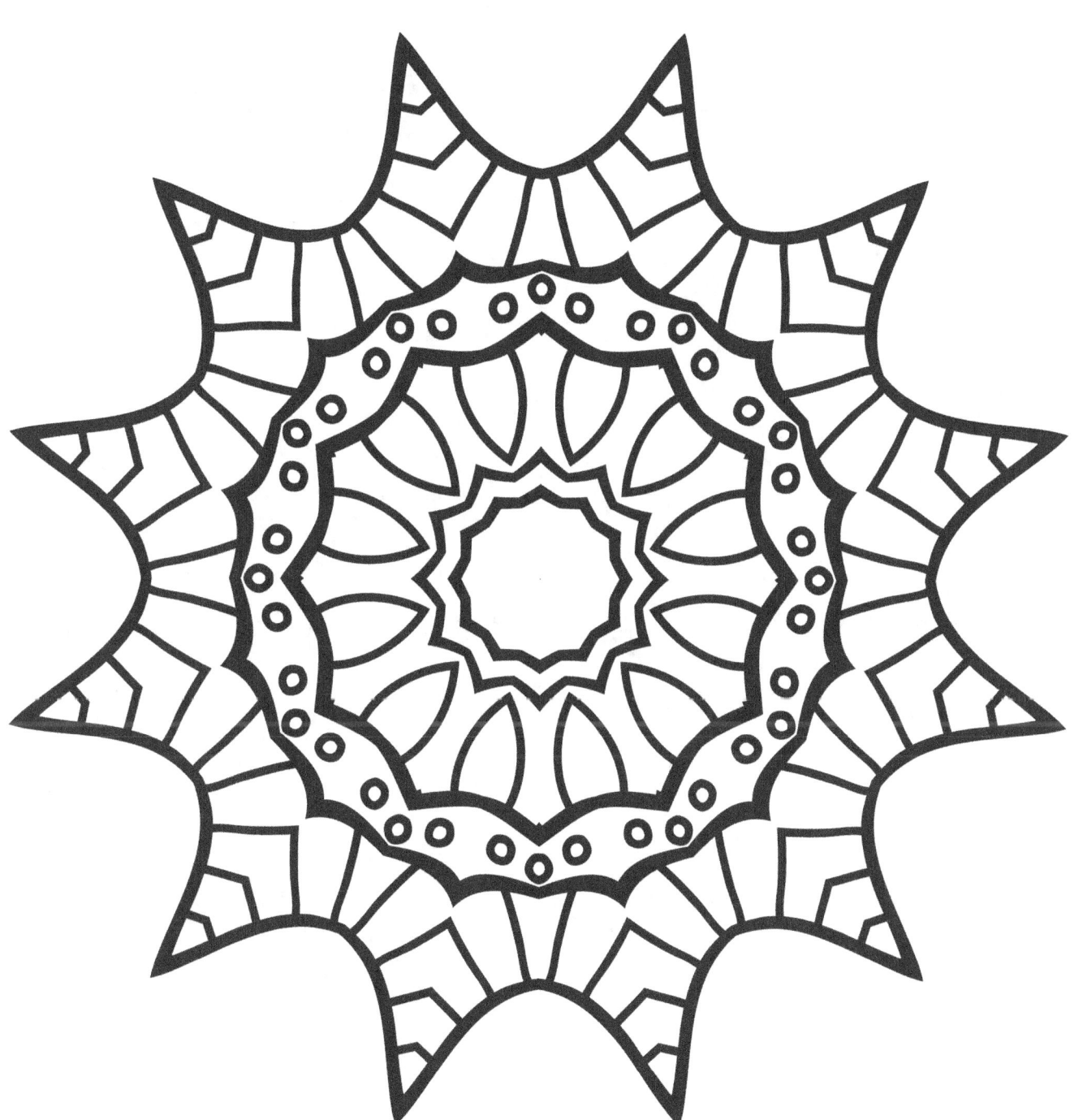

To the mind that is still,
the whole universe surrenders.

-Lao Tzu

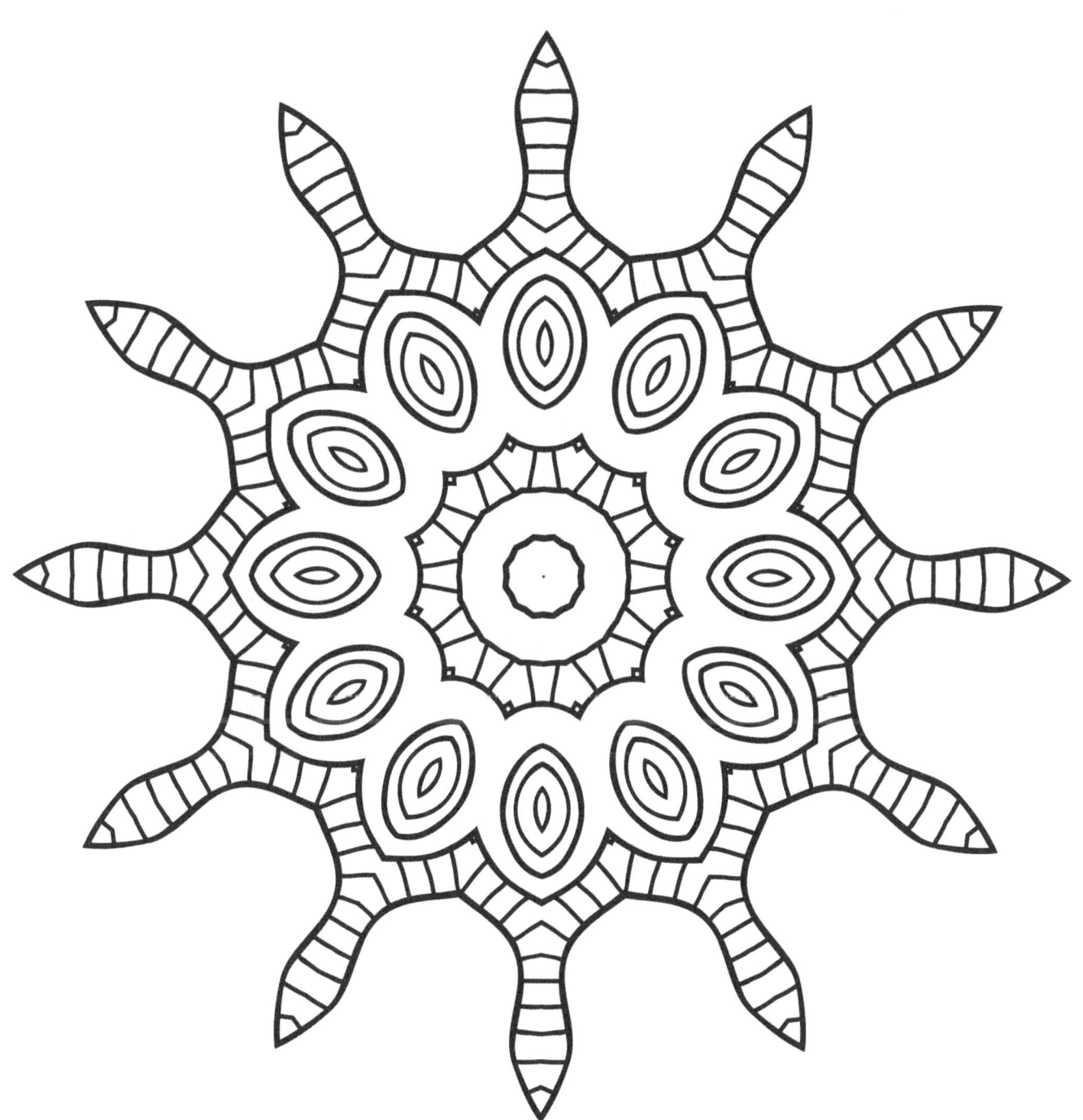

Don't judge each day by the harvest you reap
but by the seeds that you plant.

-Robert Louis Stevenson

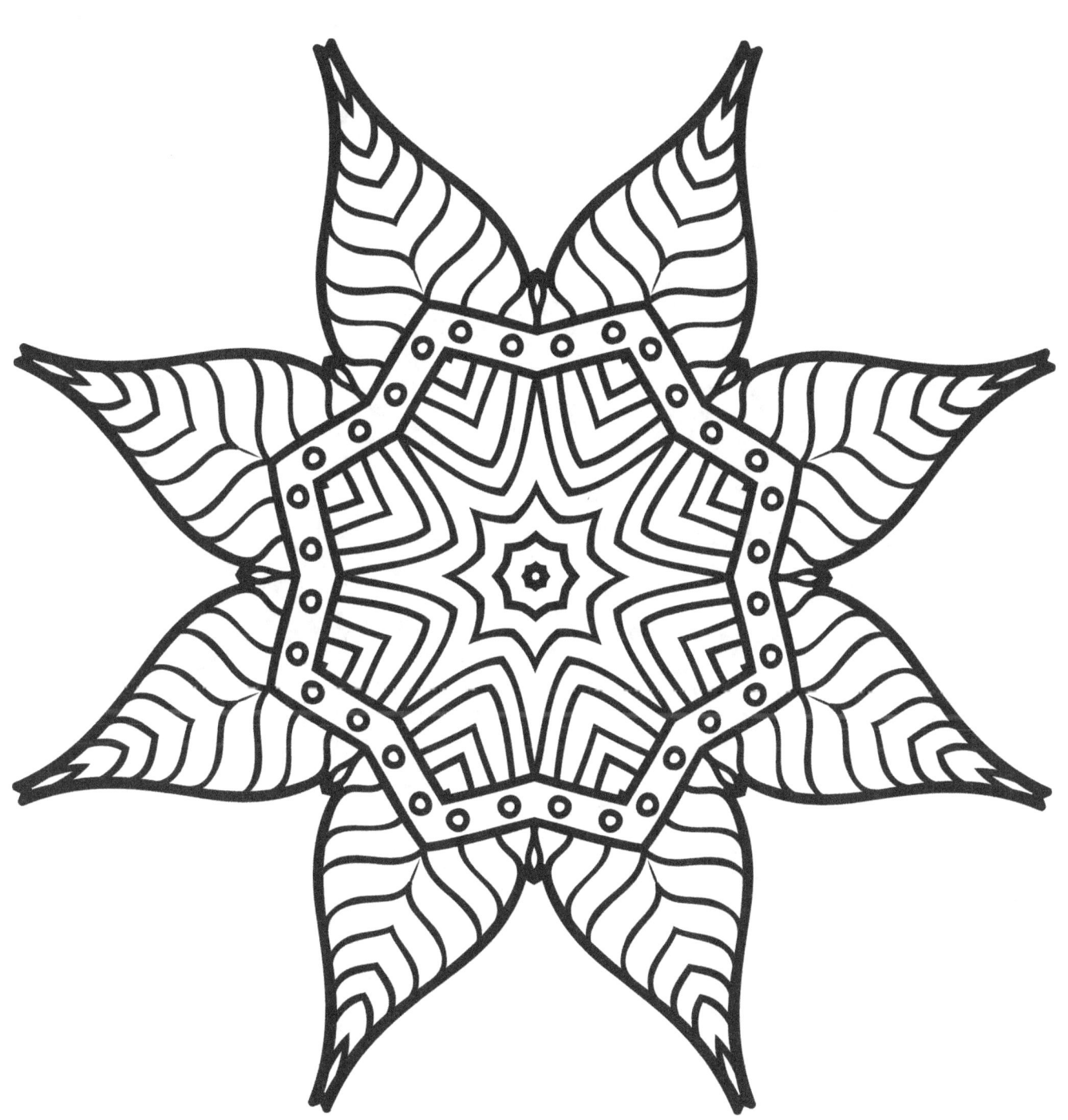

What we achieve inwardly will change outer reality.

-Plutarch

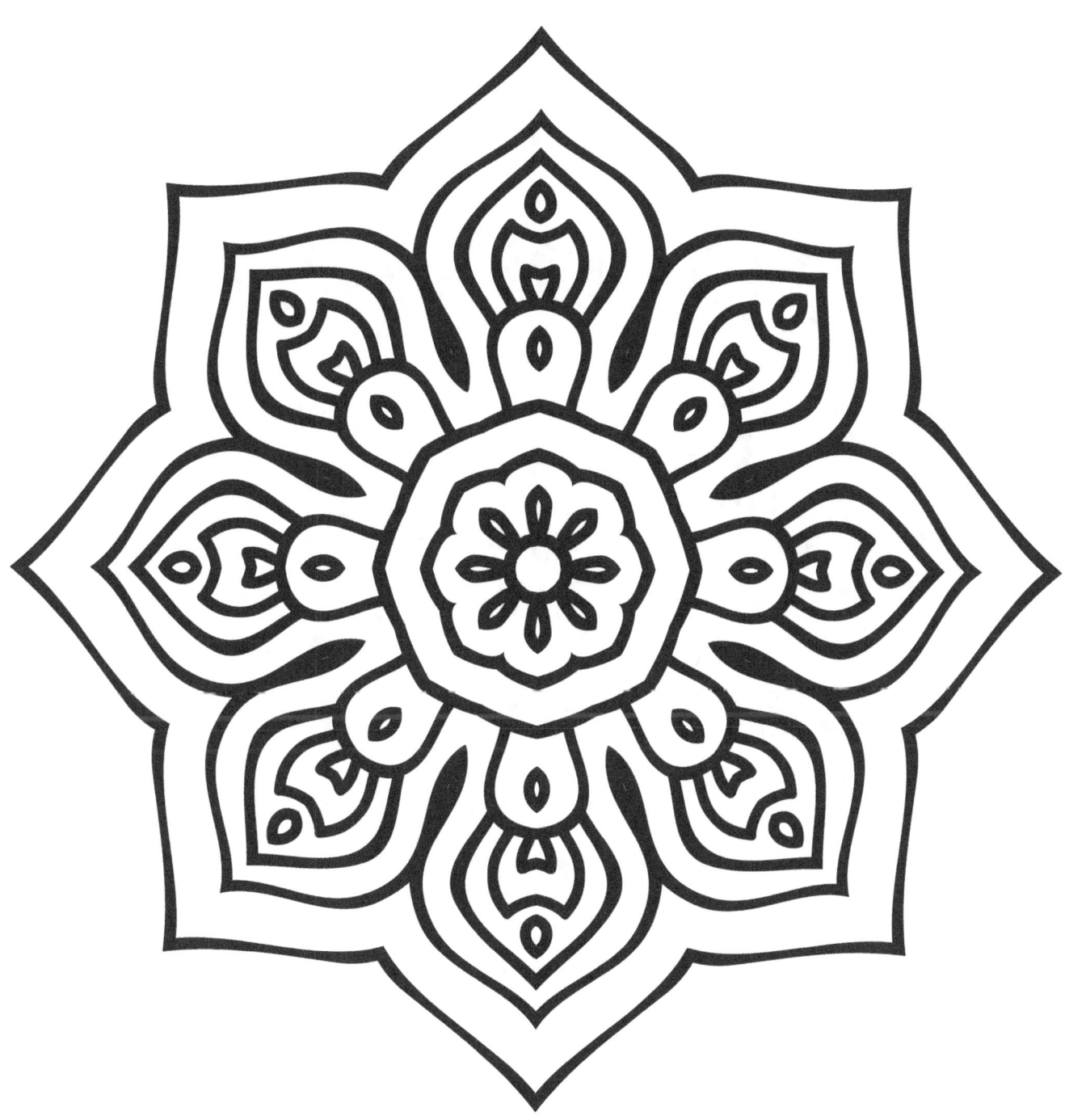

Today is the only day. Yesterday is gone.

-John Wooden

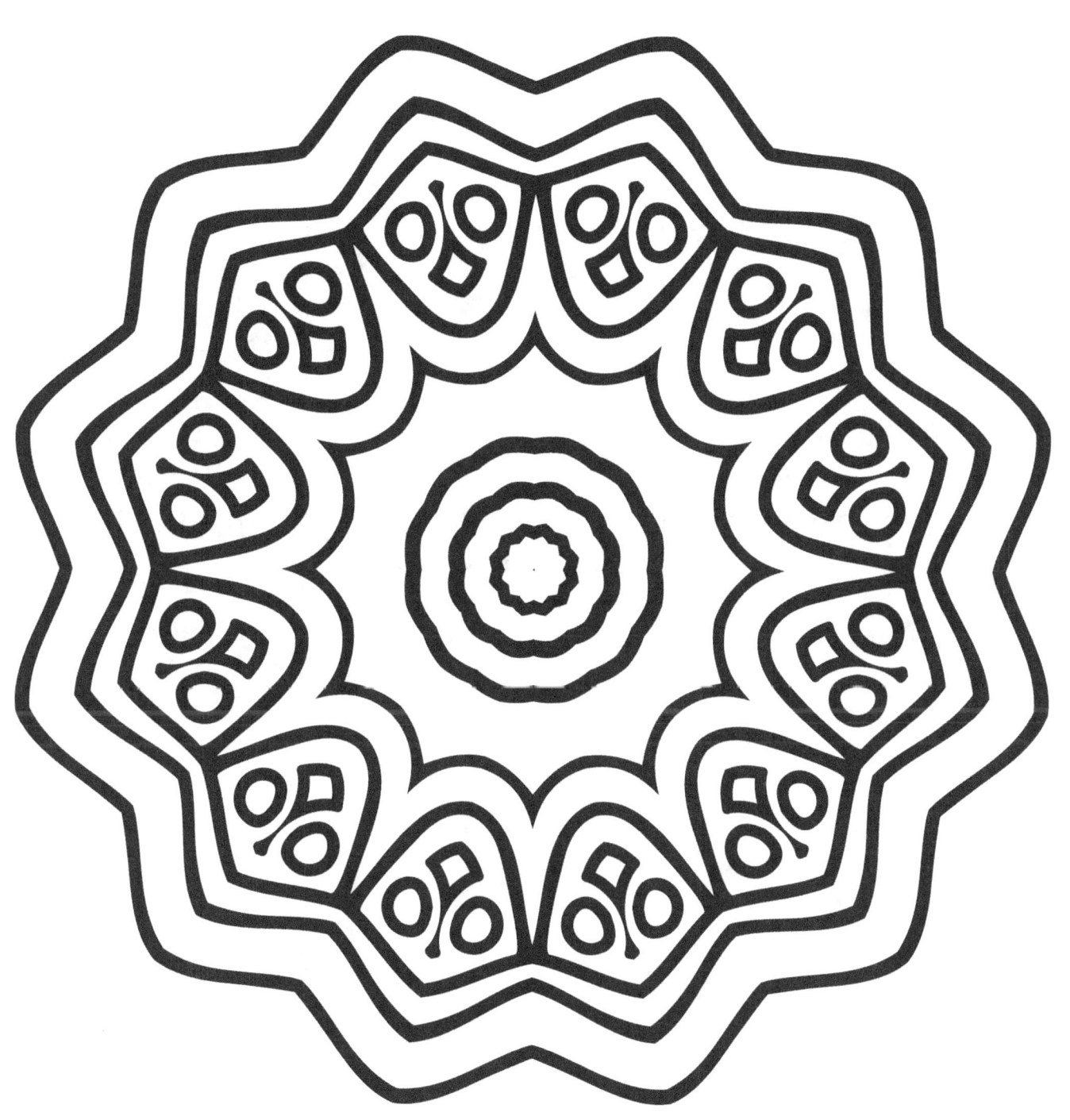

Love the moment and the energy of that moment
will spread beyond all boundaries.

-Corita Kent

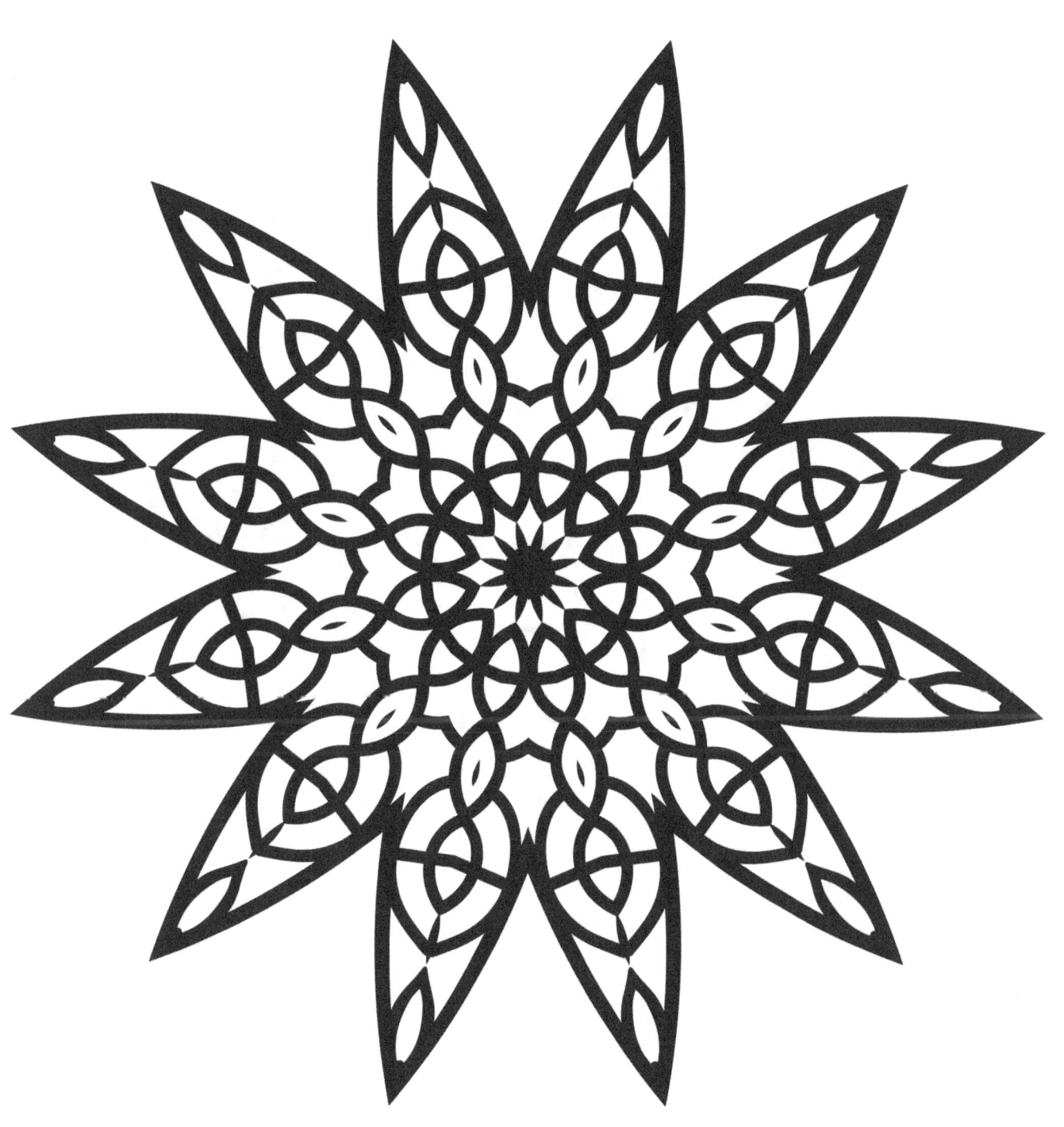

It is never too late to be what you might have been.

-George Eliot

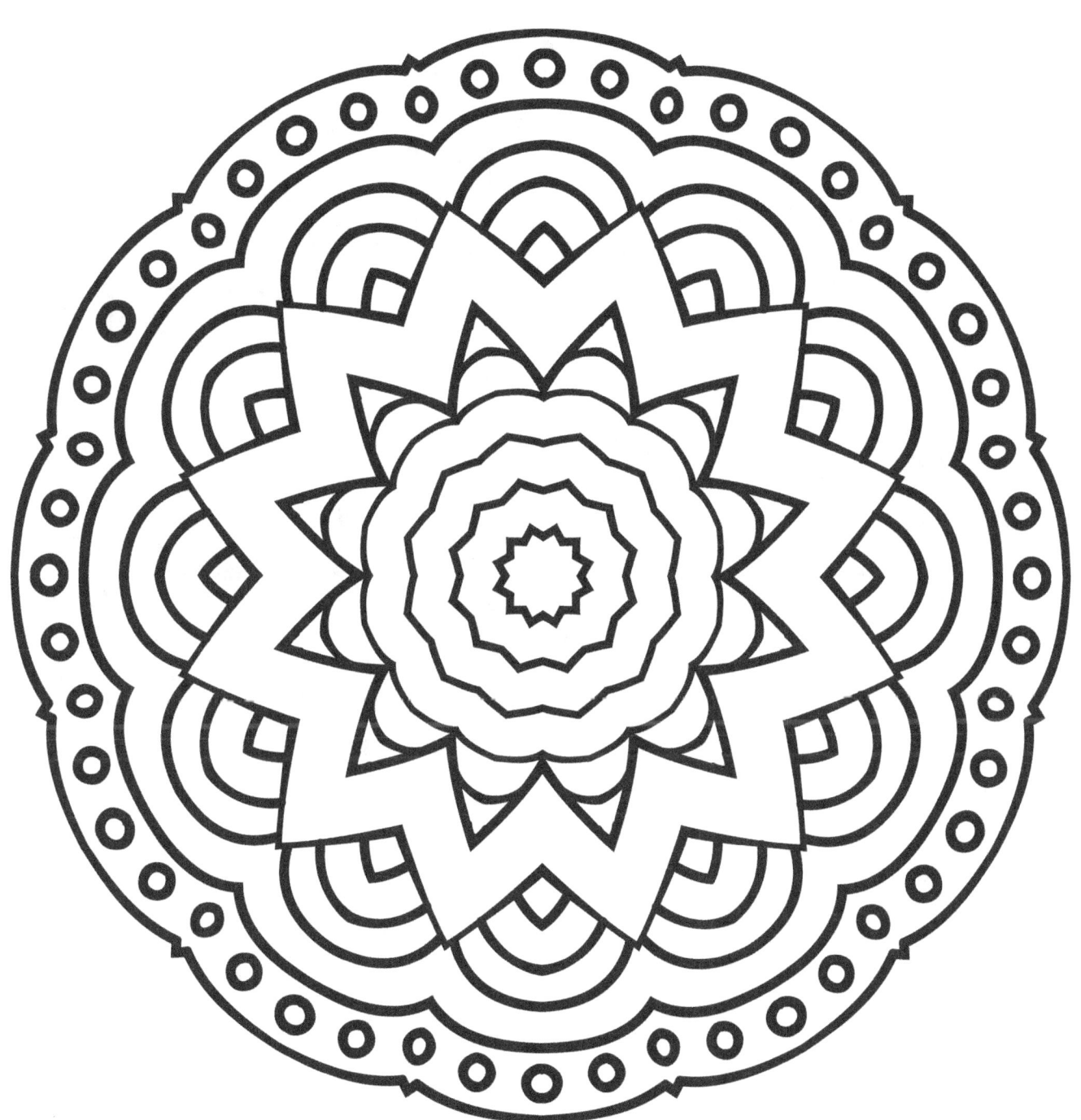

All you need is the plan, the road map, and the courage to press on to your destination.

-Earl Nightingale

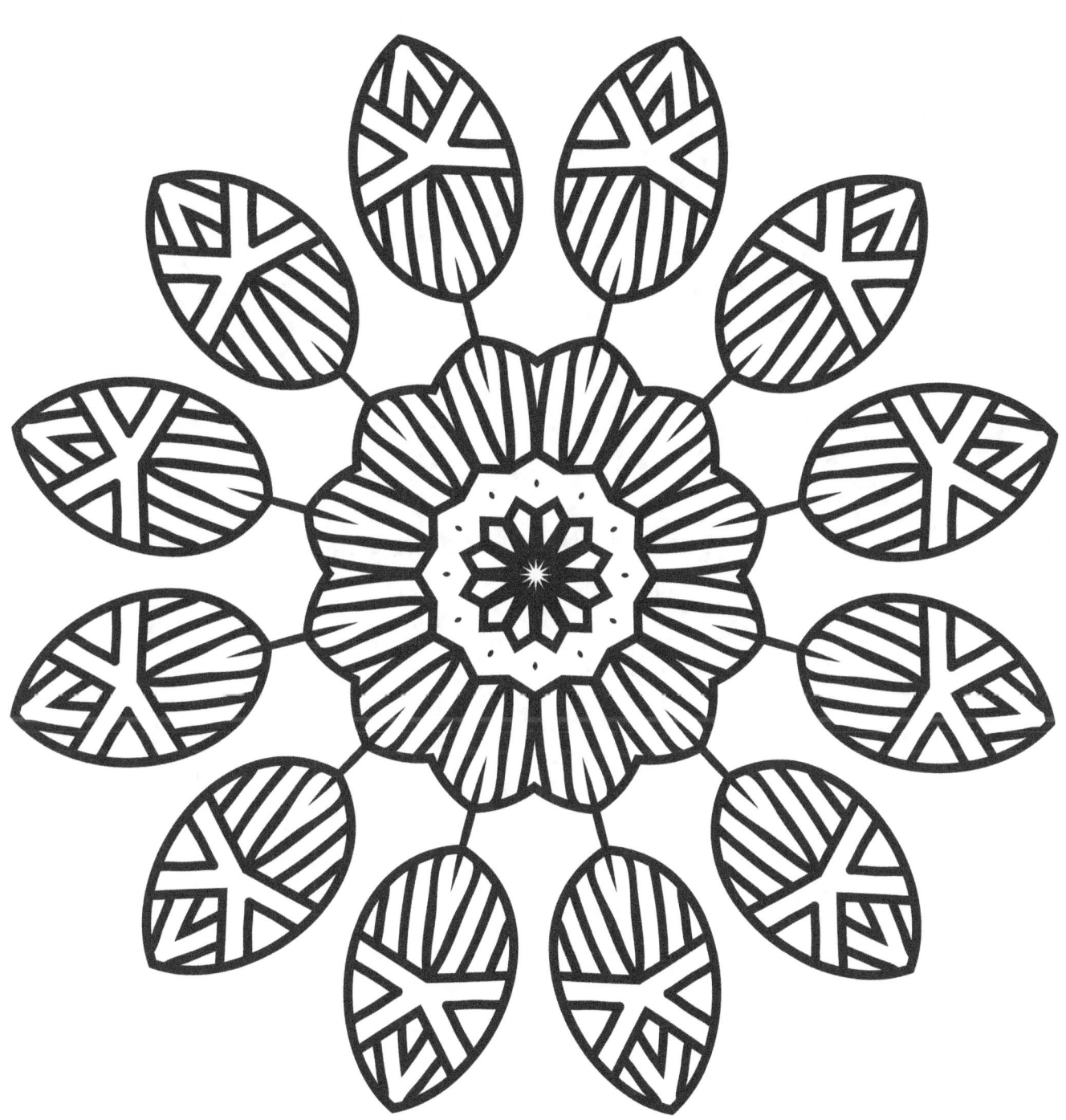

My sun sets to rise again.

-Elizabeth Barrett Browning

Your present circumstances don't determine
where you can go; they merely determine
where you start.

- Nido Qubein

Once we believe in ourselves, we can risk curiosity, wonder, spontaneous delight, or any experience that reveals the human spirit.

-E. E. Cummings

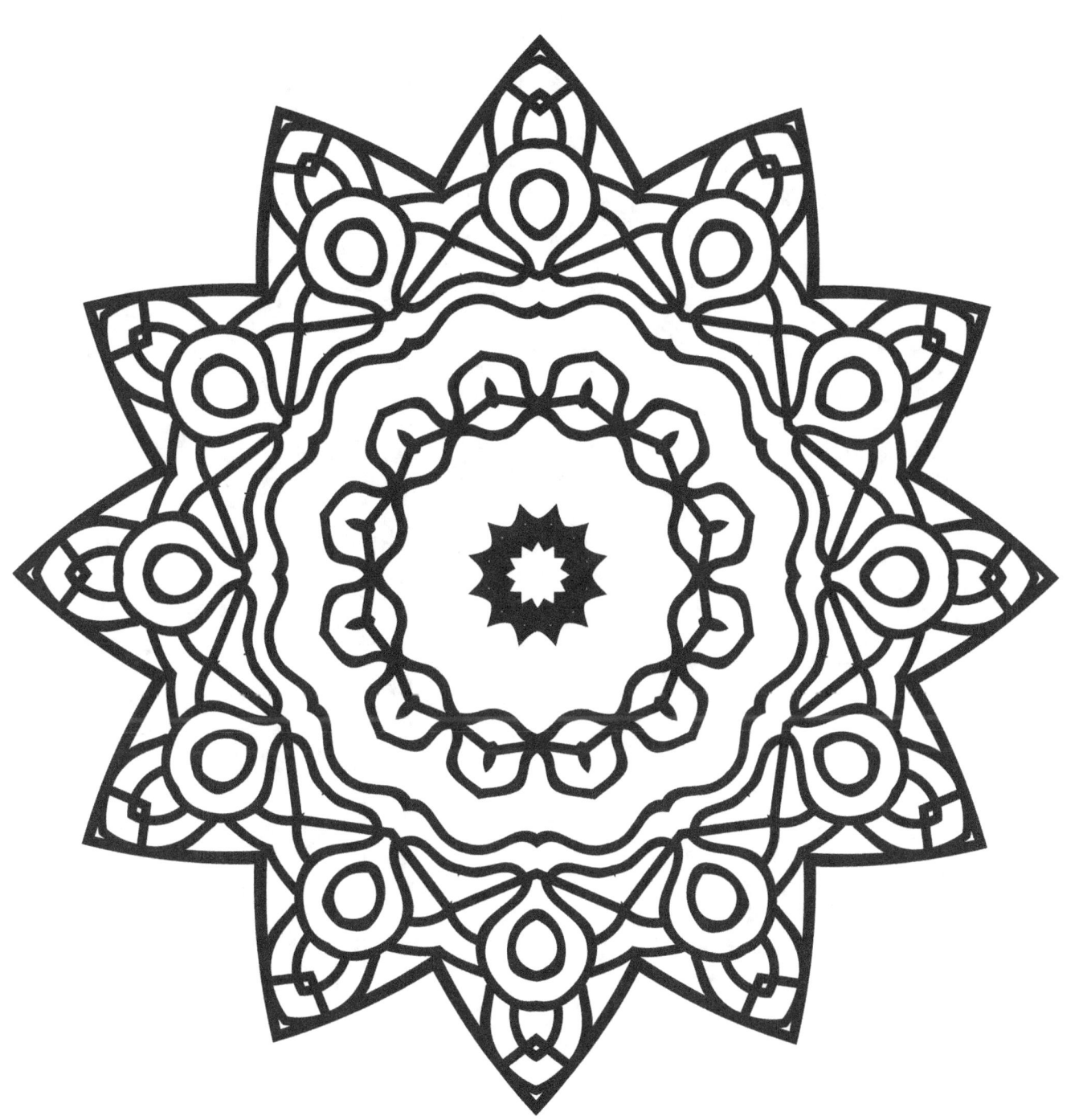

Give light, and the darkness will disappear of itself.

-Desiderius Erasmus

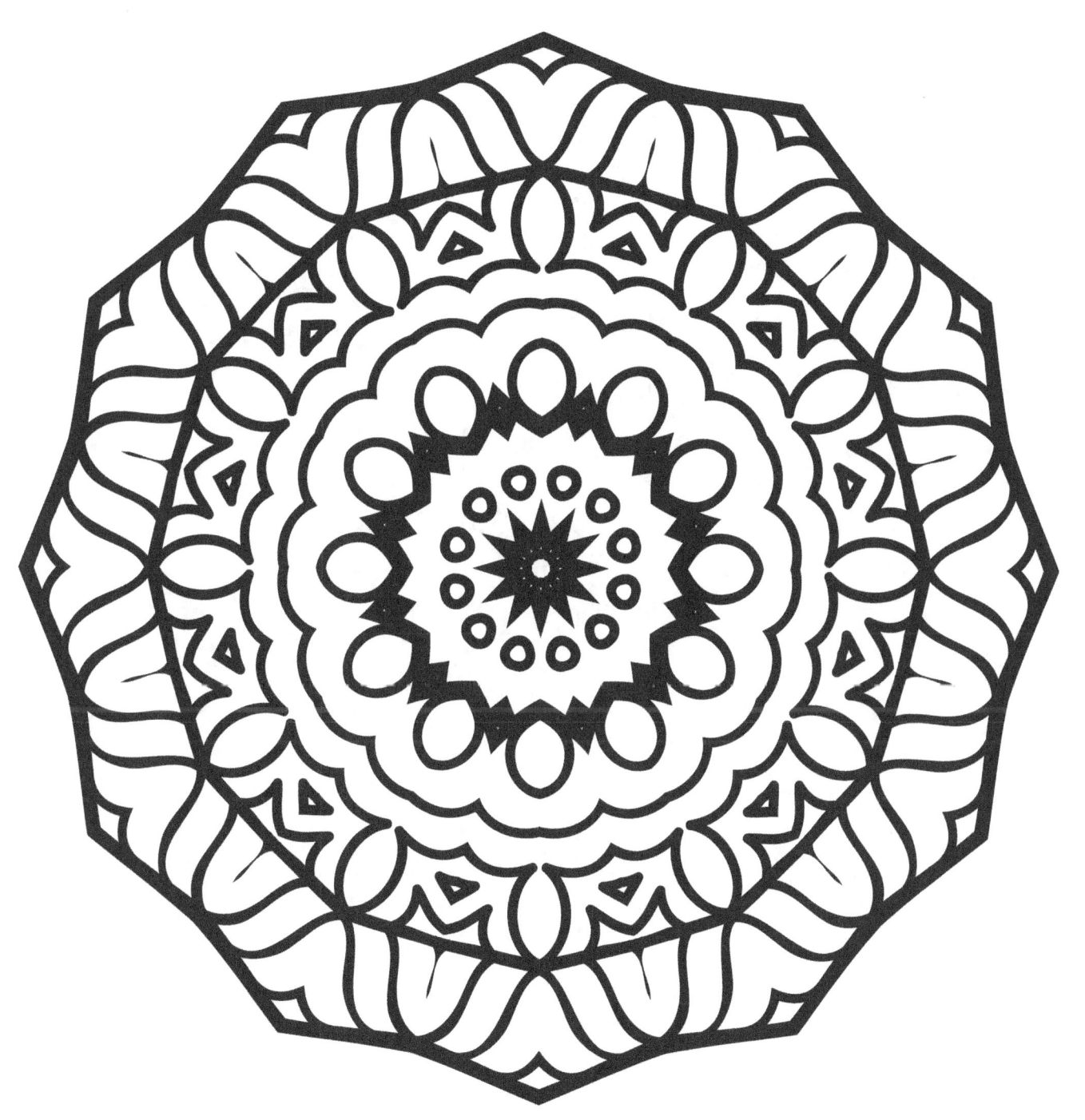

Wonder rather than doubt is
the root of all knowledge.

-Abraham Joshua Heschel

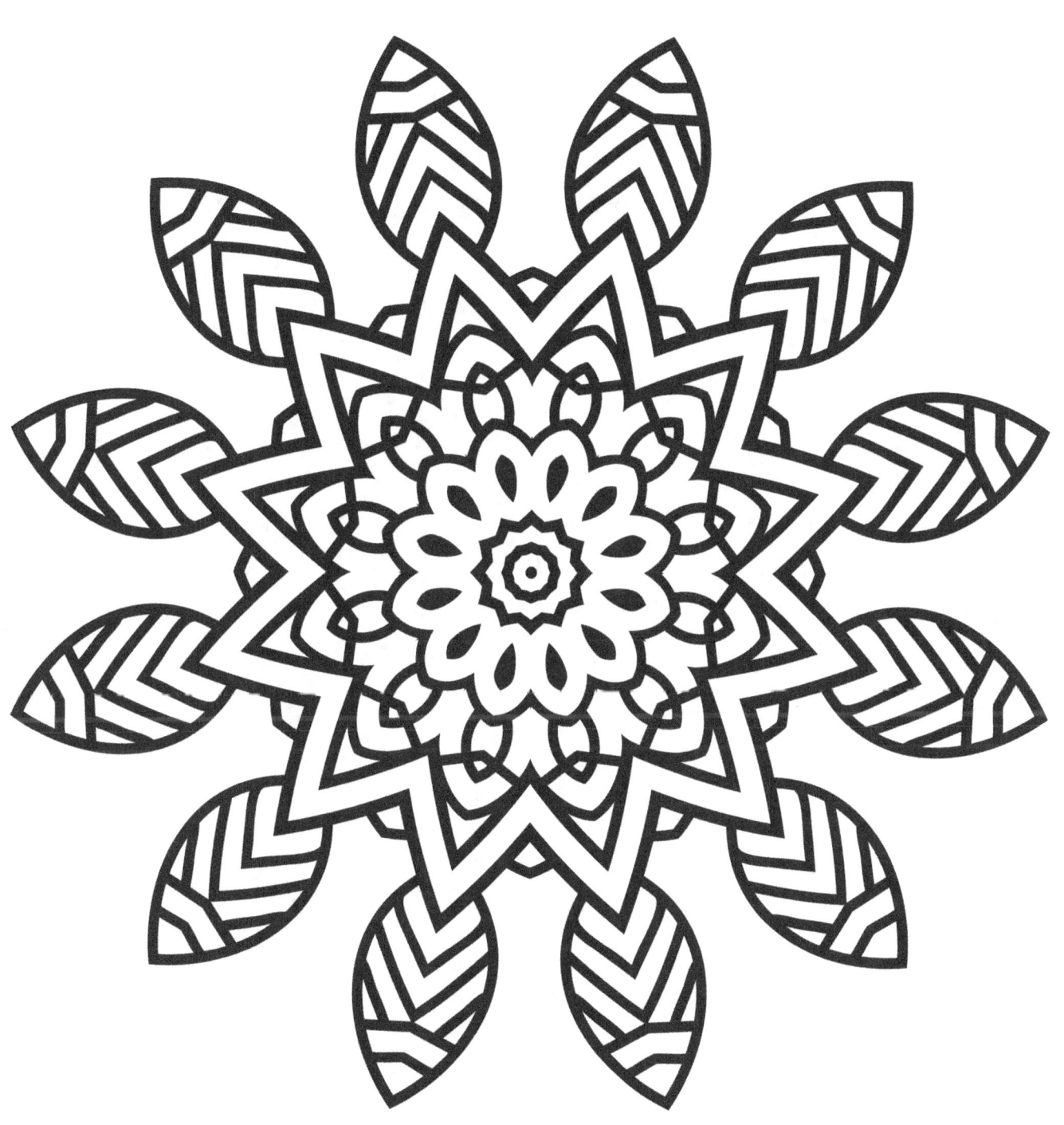

When we seek to discover the best in others,
we somehow bring out the best in ourselves.

-William Arthur Ward

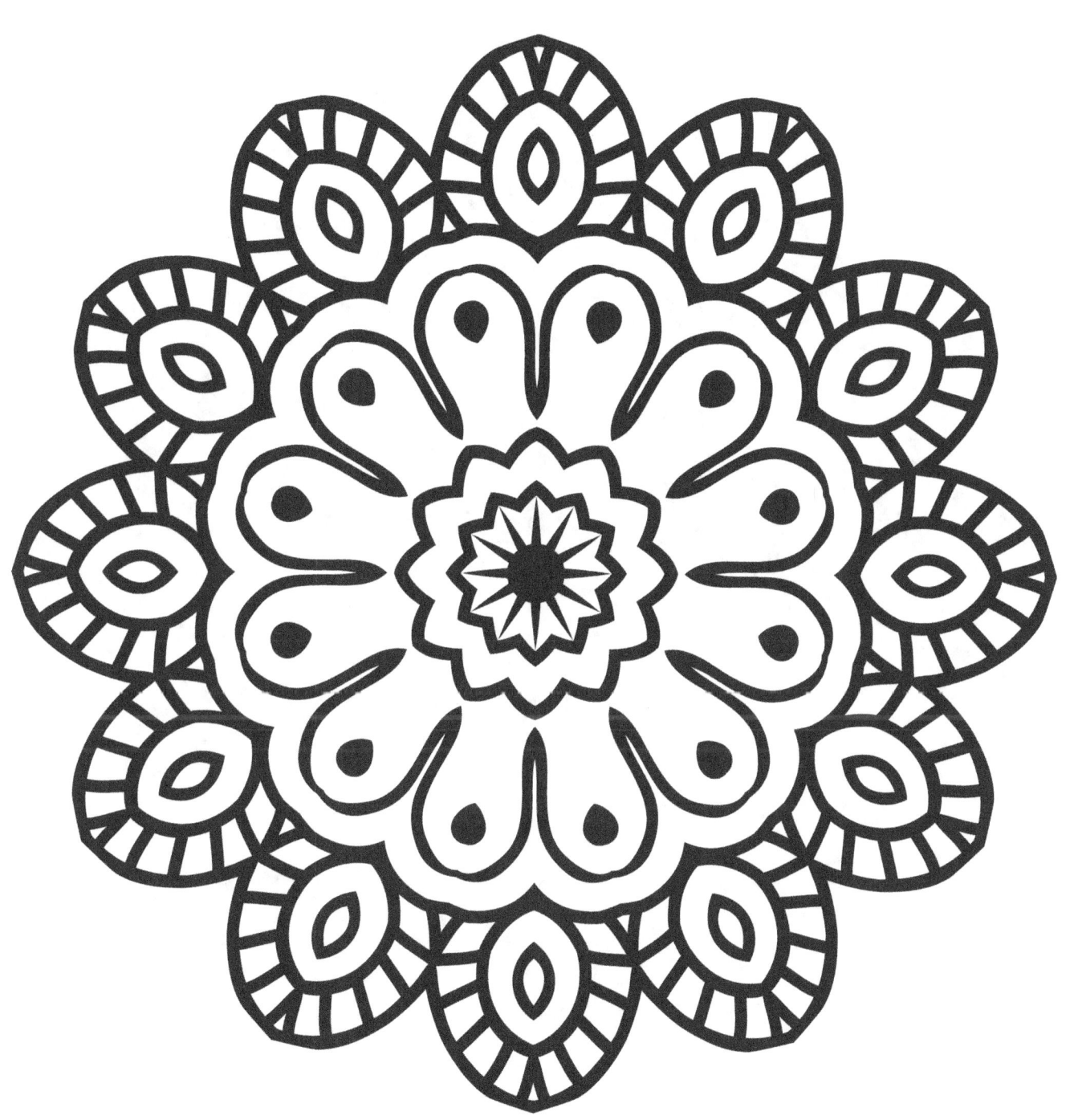

Vitality shows in not only the ability to persist
but the ability to start over.

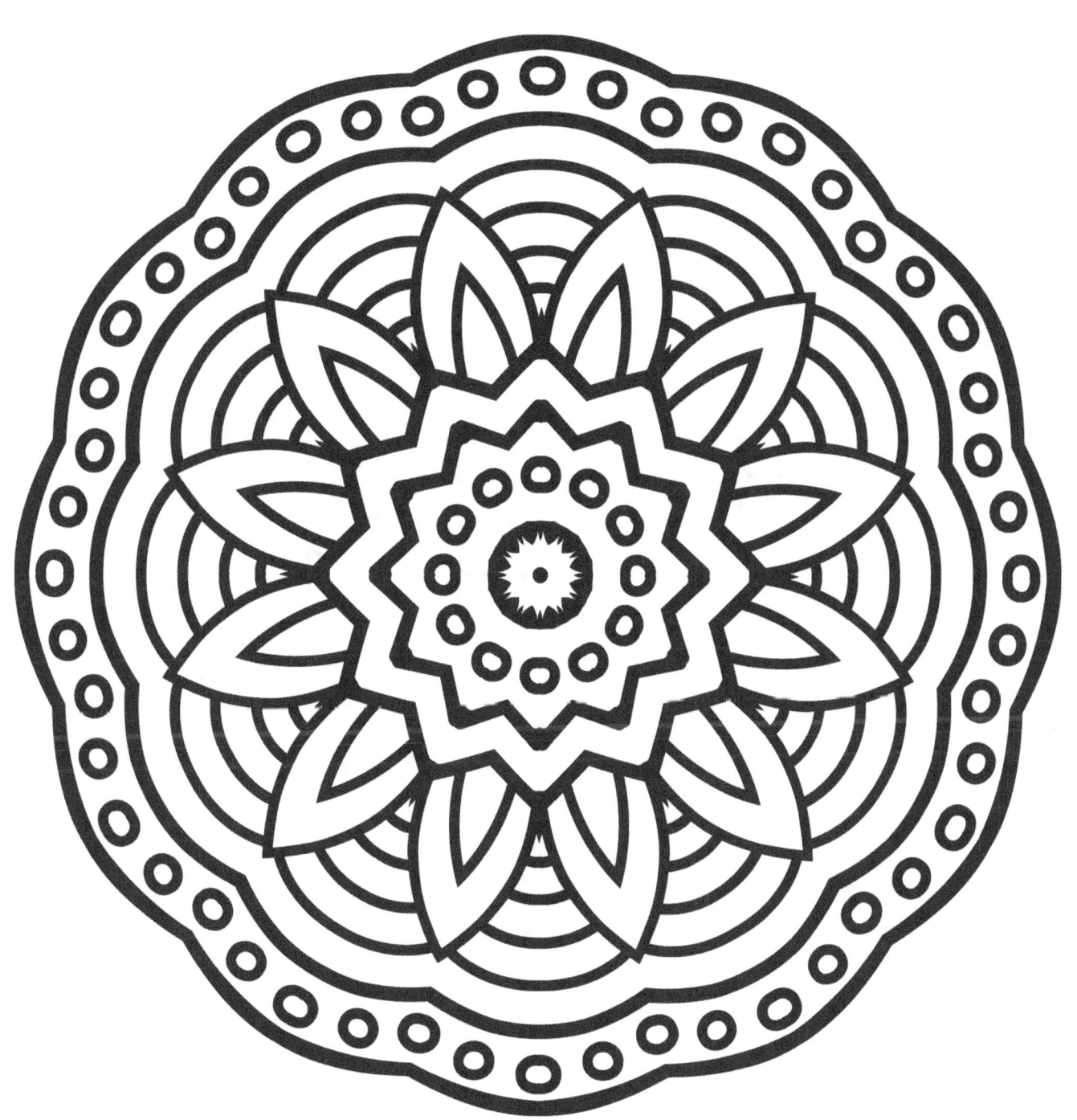

You are always free to change your mind and choose a different future, or a different past.

-Richard Bach

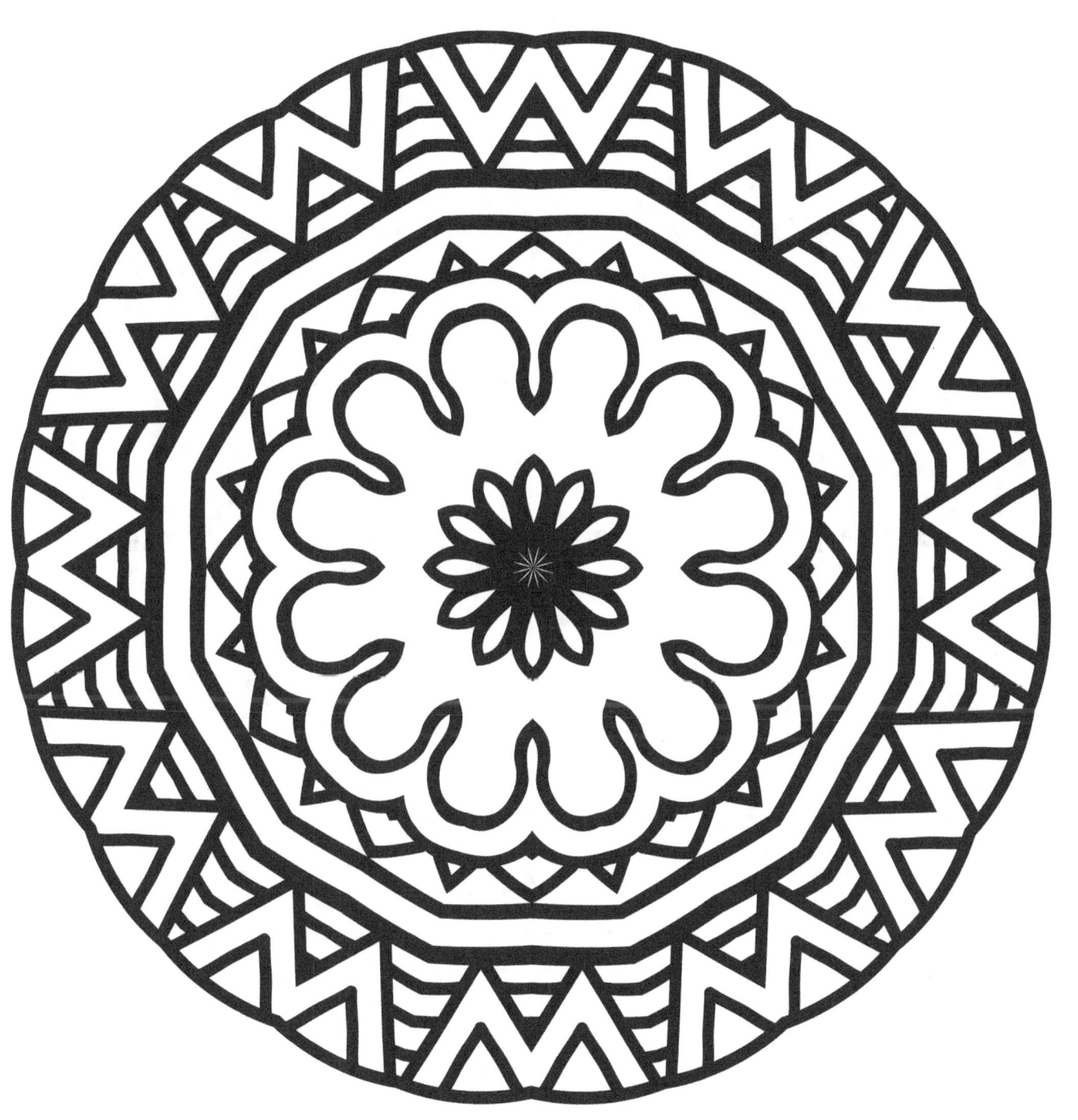

A #2 pencil and a dream can take you anywhere.

-Joyce Meyer

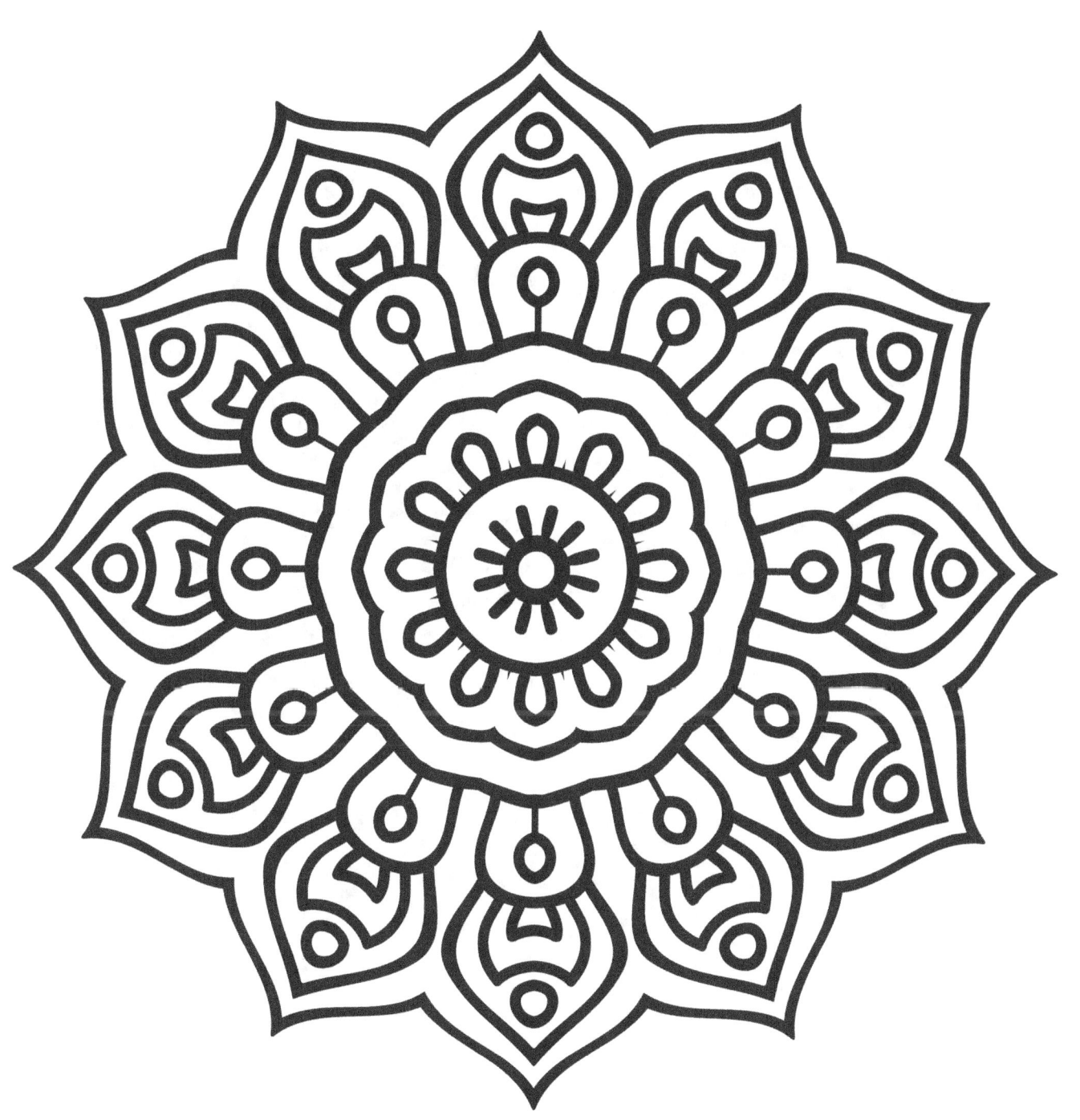

I am not afraid of tomorrow, for I have seen
yesterday and I love today!

-William Allen White

Find out who you are and be that person. That's what your soul was put on this Earth to be. Find that truth, live that truth and everything else will come.

-Ellen DeGeneres

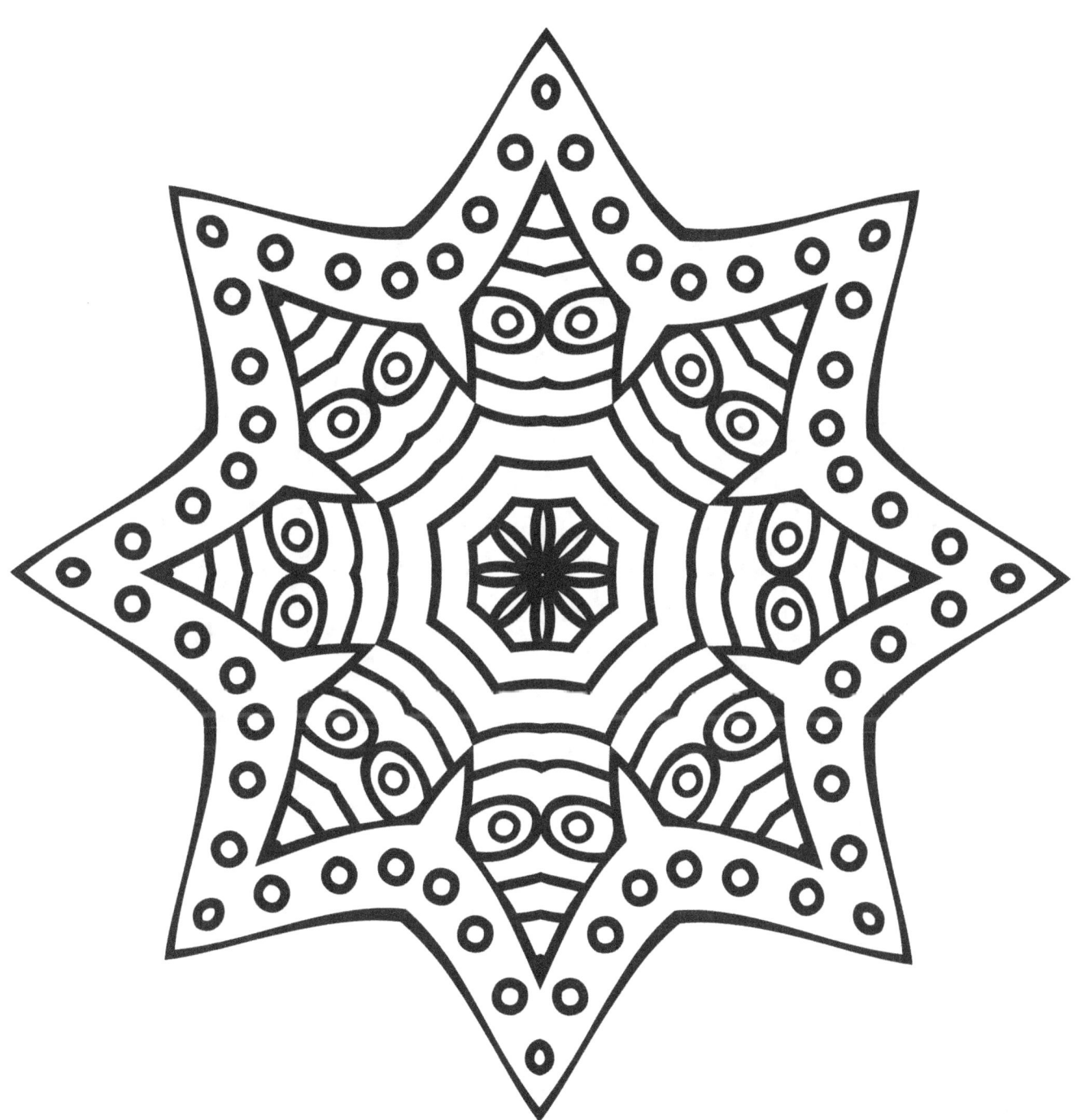

We relish news of our heroes, forgetting that
we are extraordinary to somebody too.

-Helen Hayes

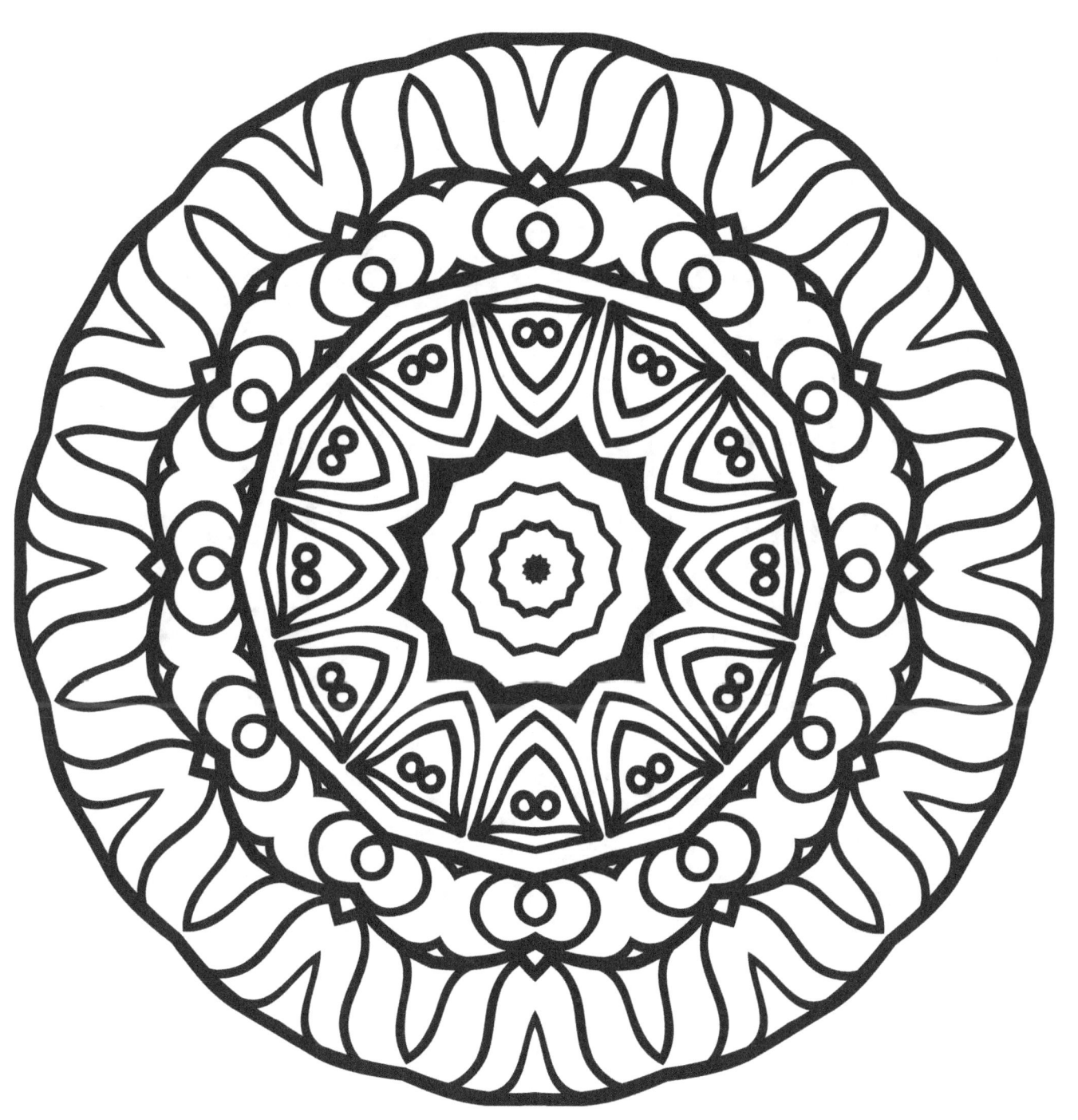

When you have a dream, you've got to grab it
and never let go.

-Carol Burnett

I believe that if one always looked at the skies,
one would end up with wings.

-Gustave Flaubert

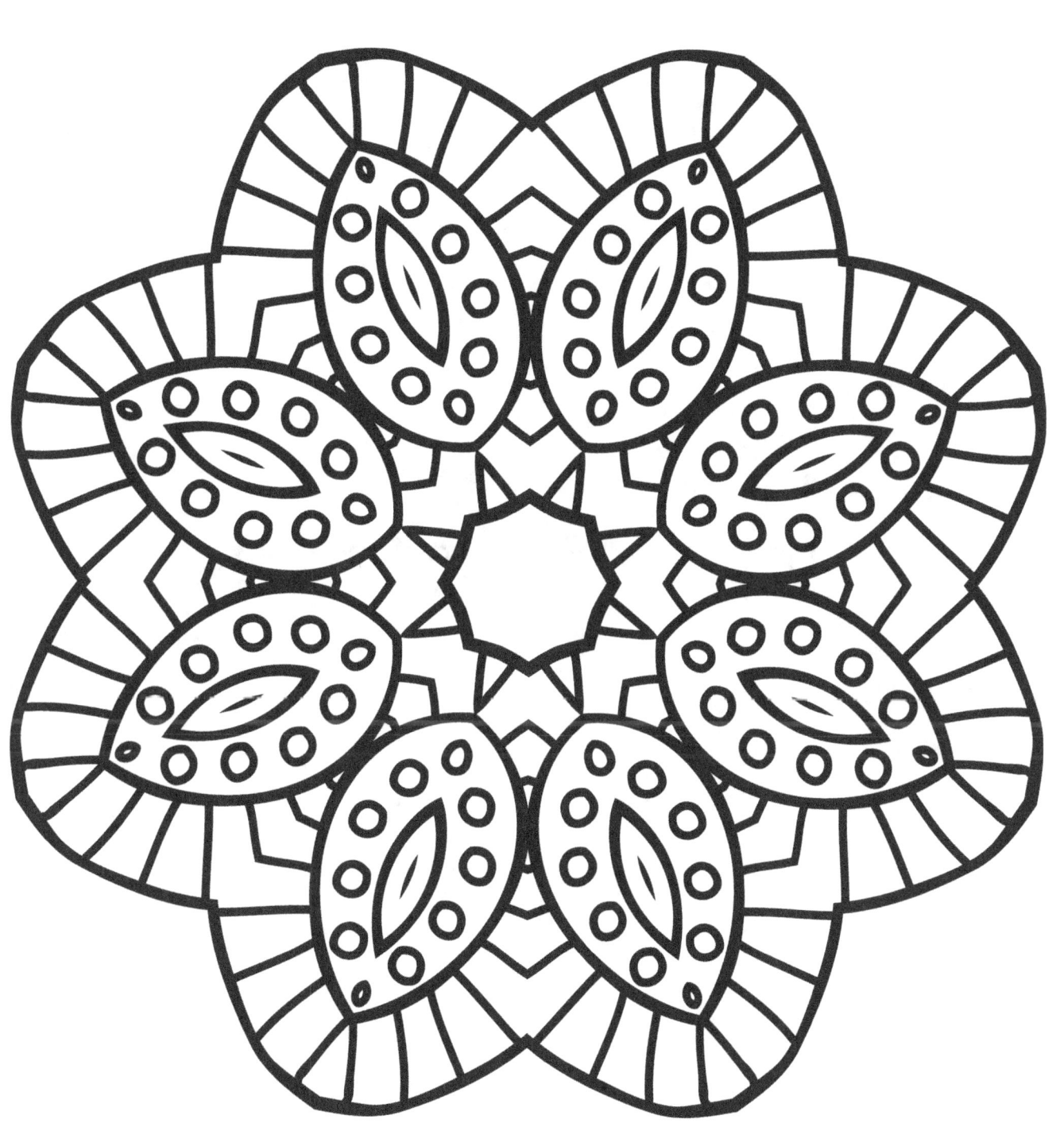

One today is worth two tomorrows.

-Benjamin Franklin

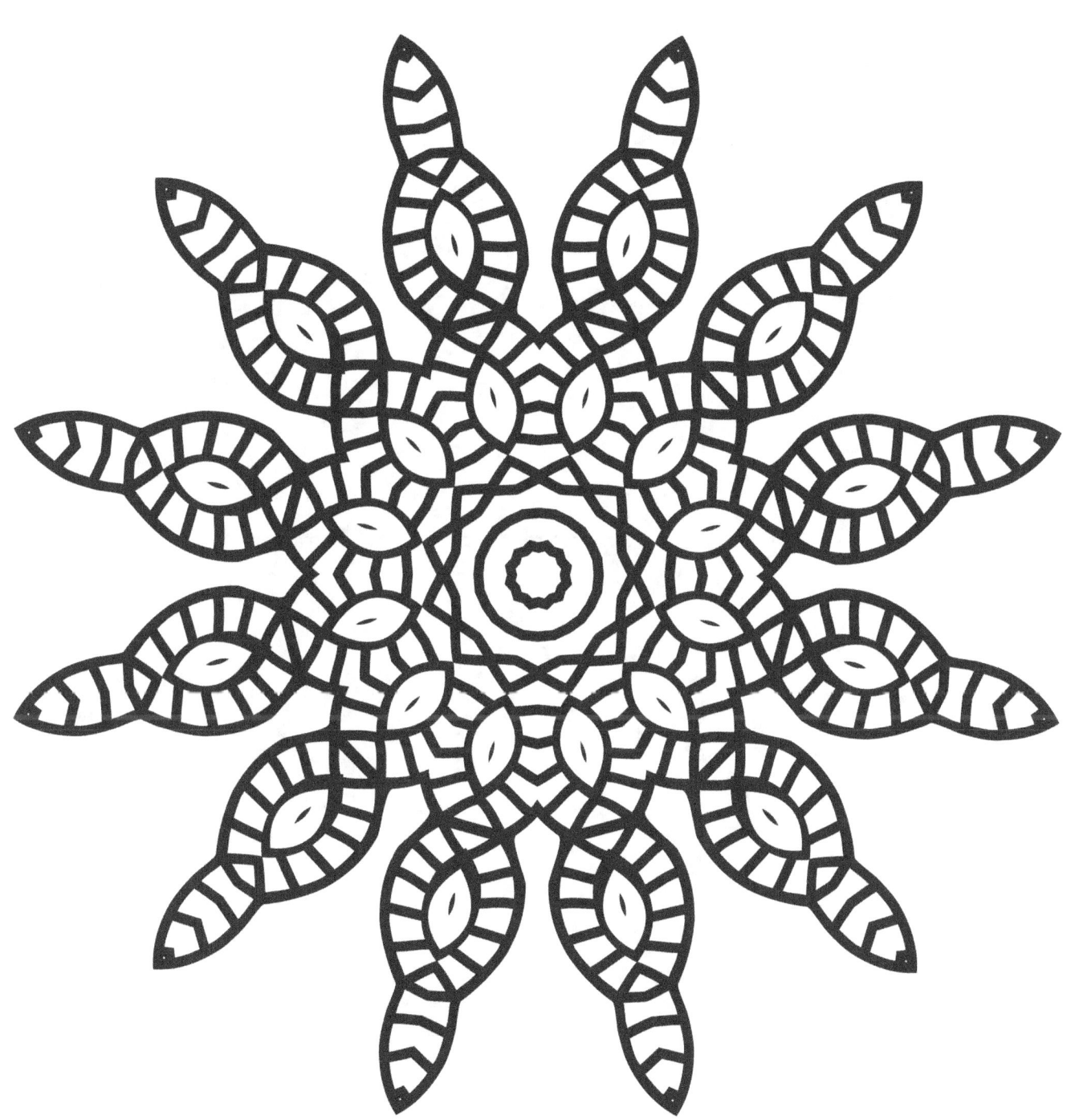

I am deliberate and afraid of nothing.

-Audre Lorde

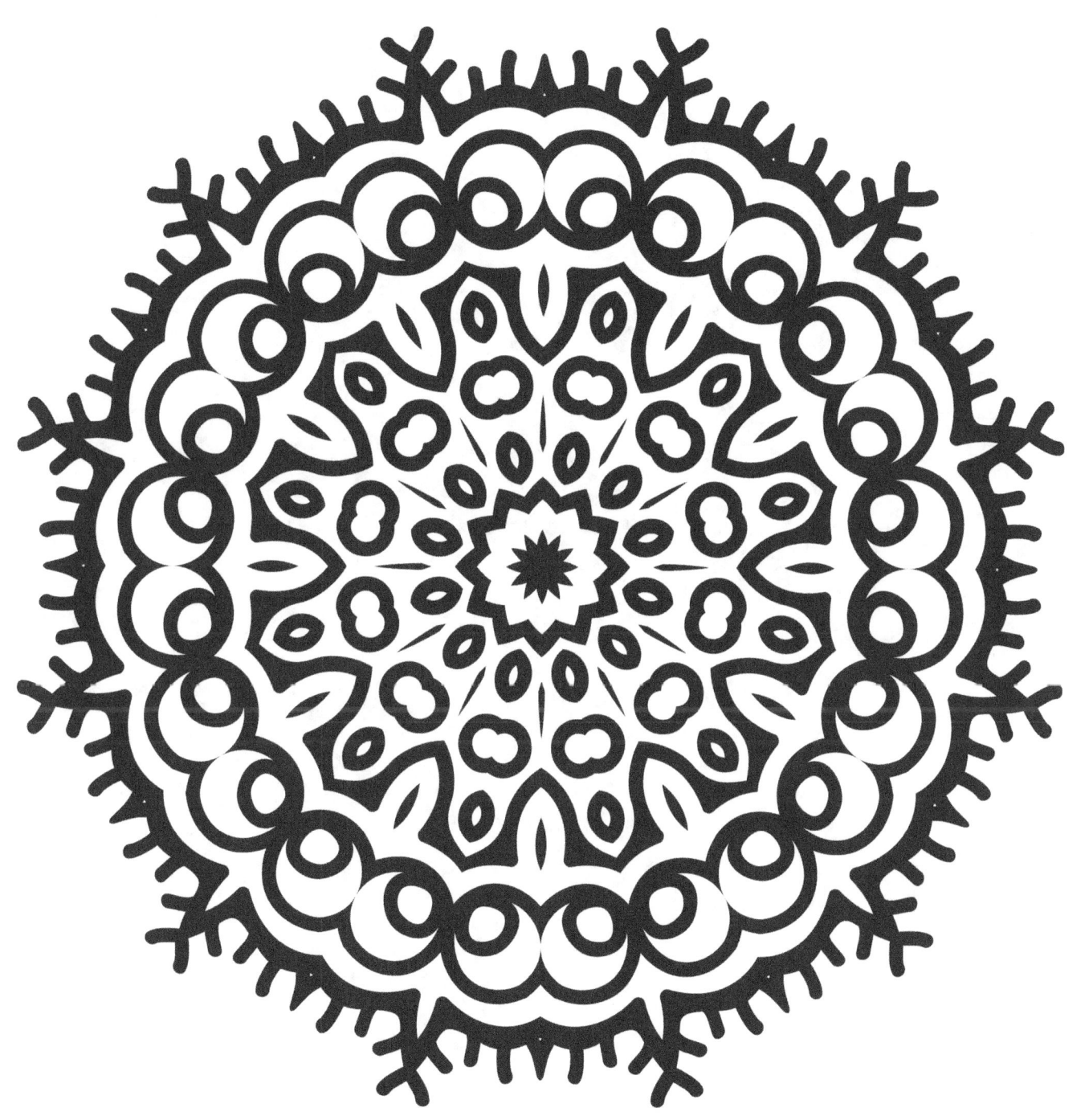

Thinking: the talking of the soul with itself.

-Plato

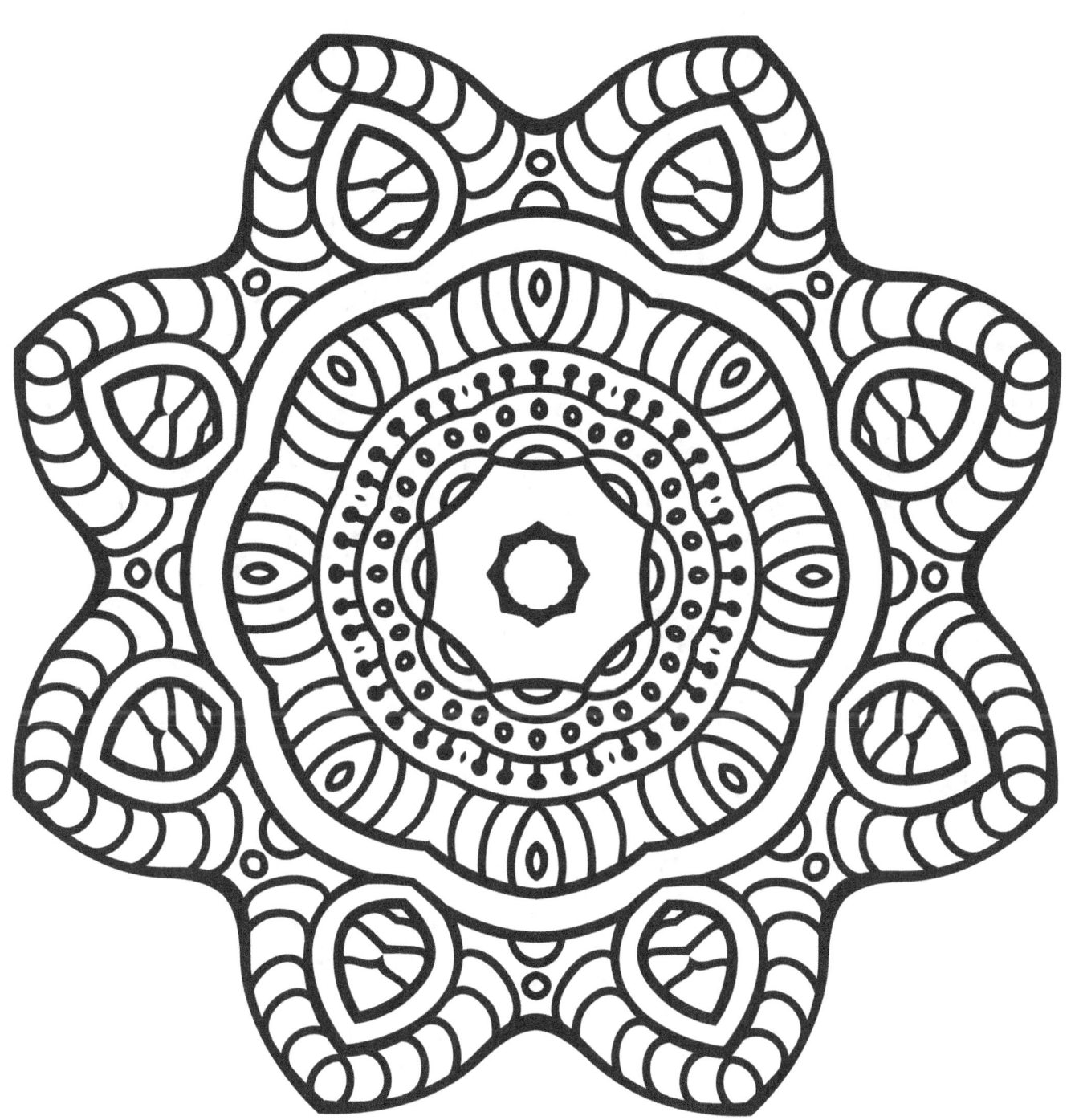

I think anyone who has a passion for what they
love to do, and who pursue it,
is inspirational for me.

-Colin Morgan

Aim for the moon. If you miss, you may hit a star.

-W. Clement Stone

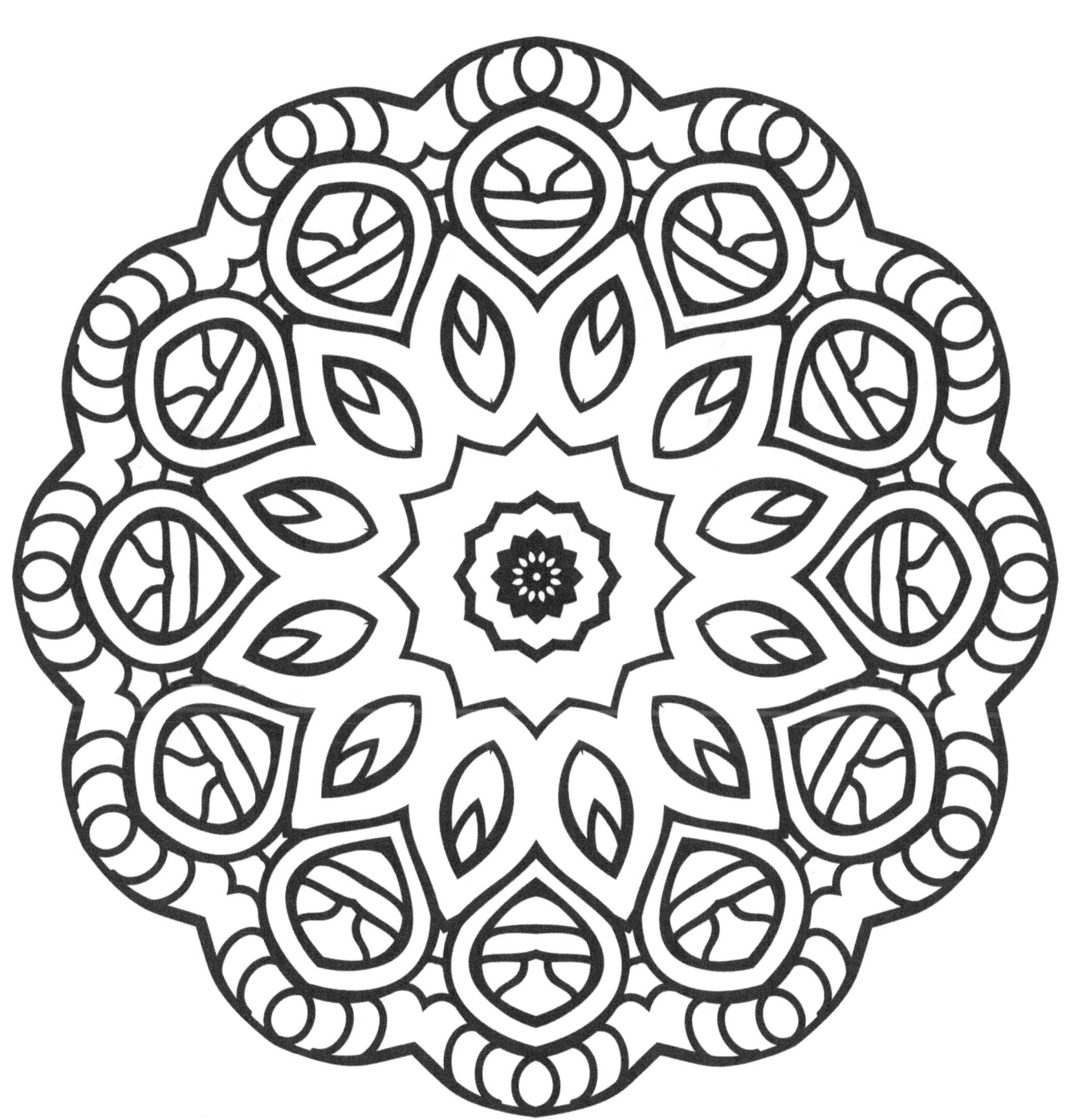

Don't watch the clock; do what it does. Keep going.

-Sam Levenson

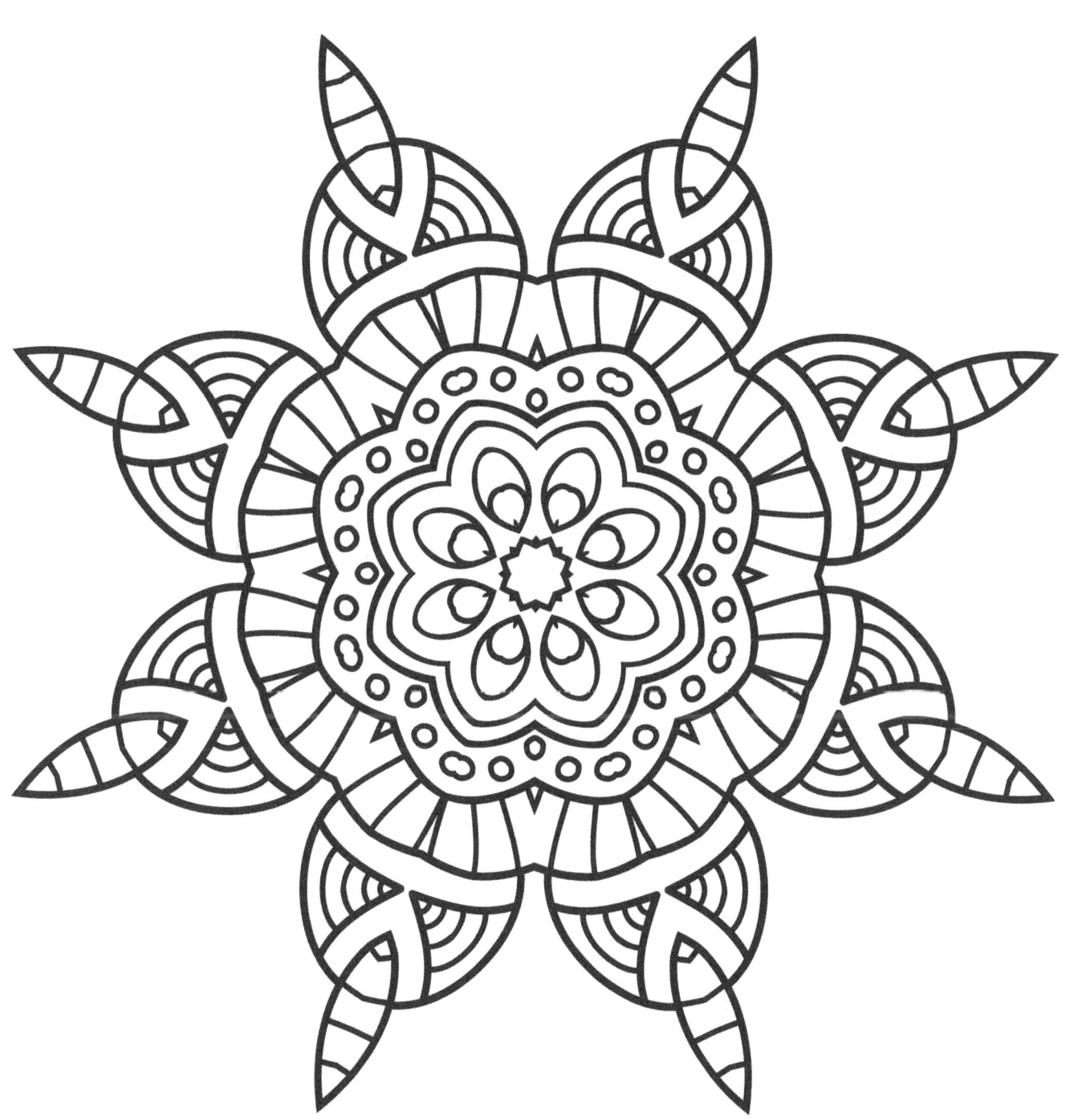

The secret of getting ahead is getting started.

-Mark Twain

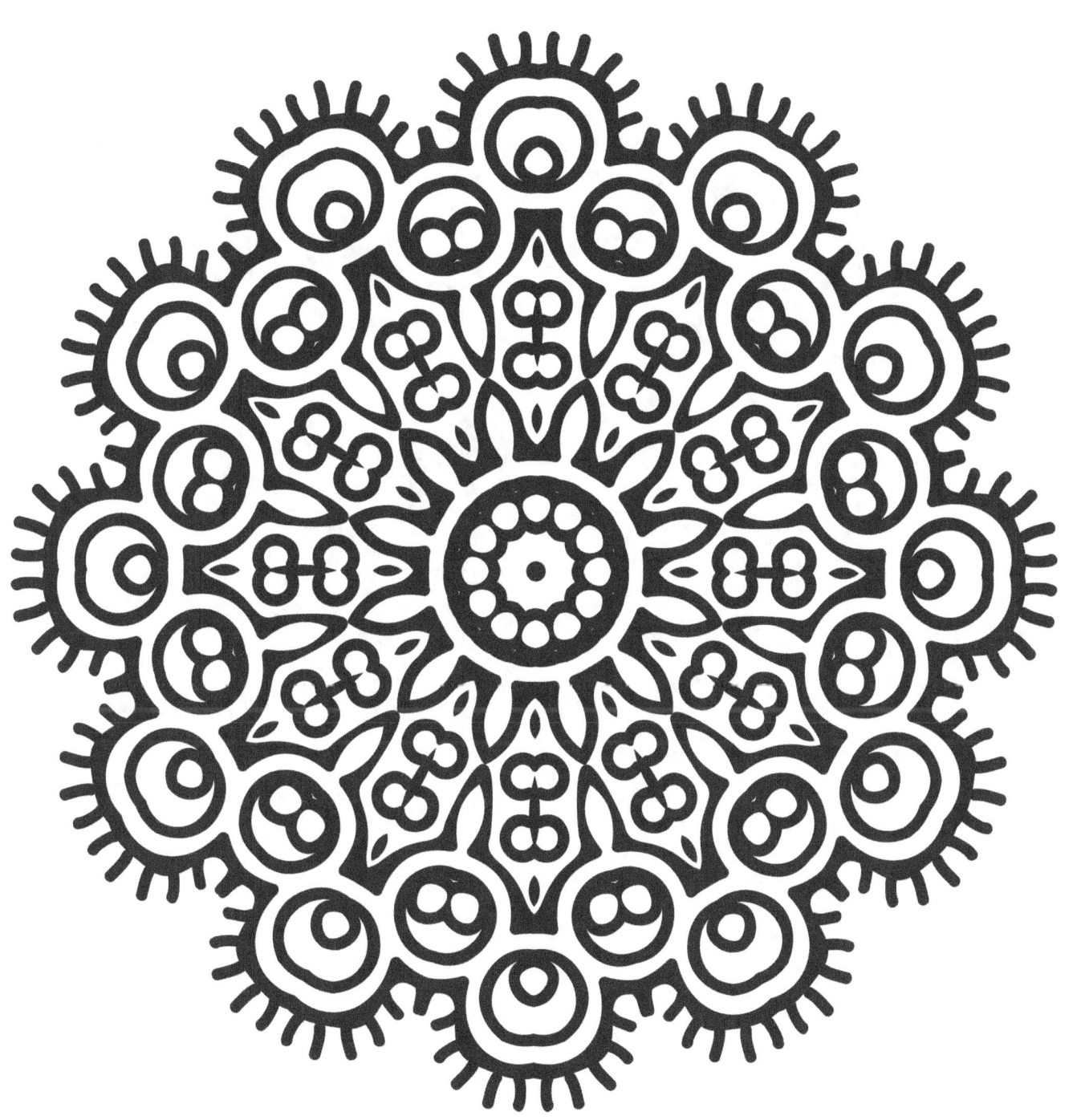

It does not matter how slowly you go as long as
you do not stop.

-Confucius

With the new day comes new strength and
new thoughts.

-Eleanor Roosevelt

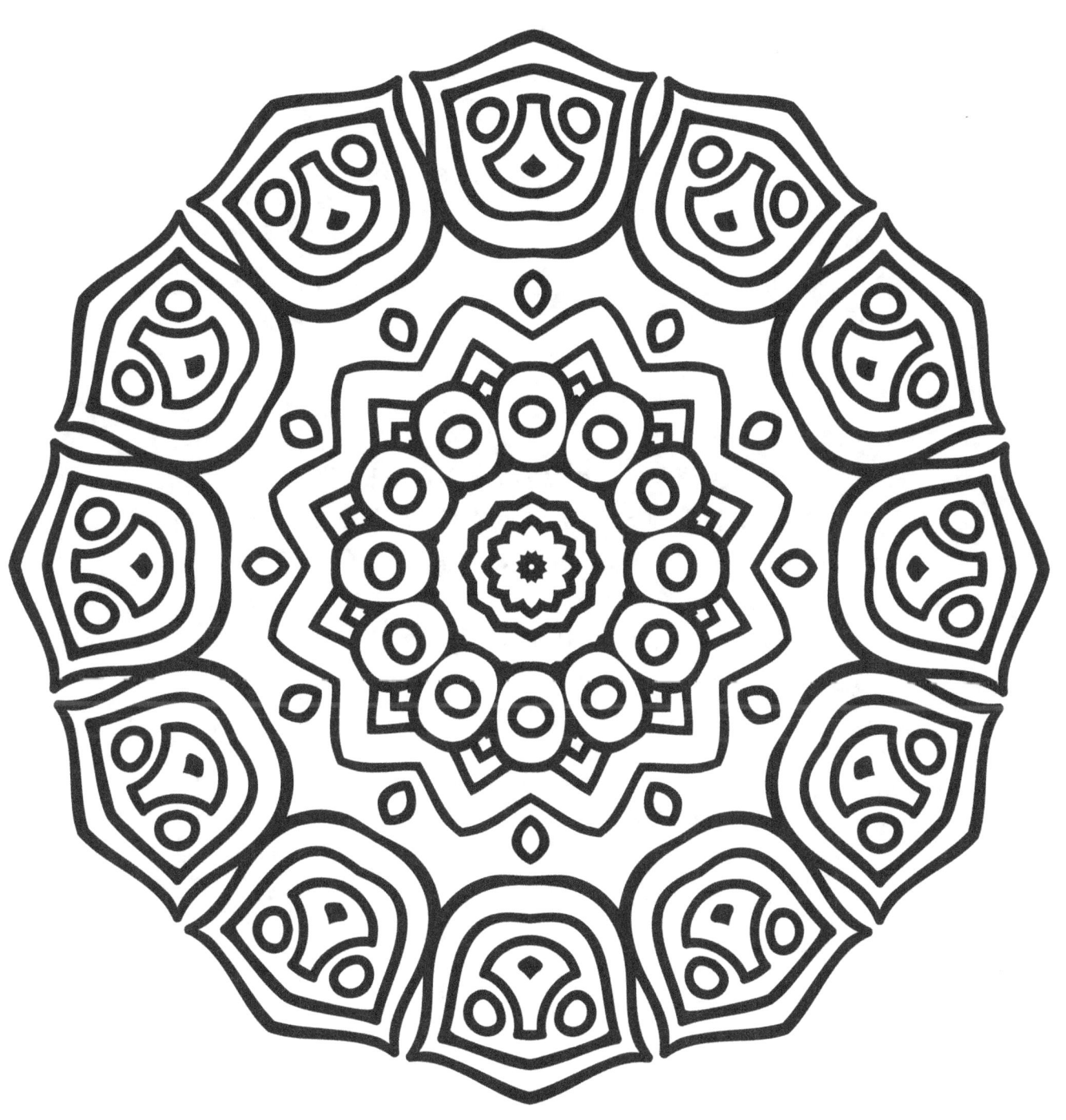

Believe in yourself! Have faith in your abilities!
Without a humble but reasonable confidence
in your own powers you cannot be
successful or happy.

-Norman Vincent Peale

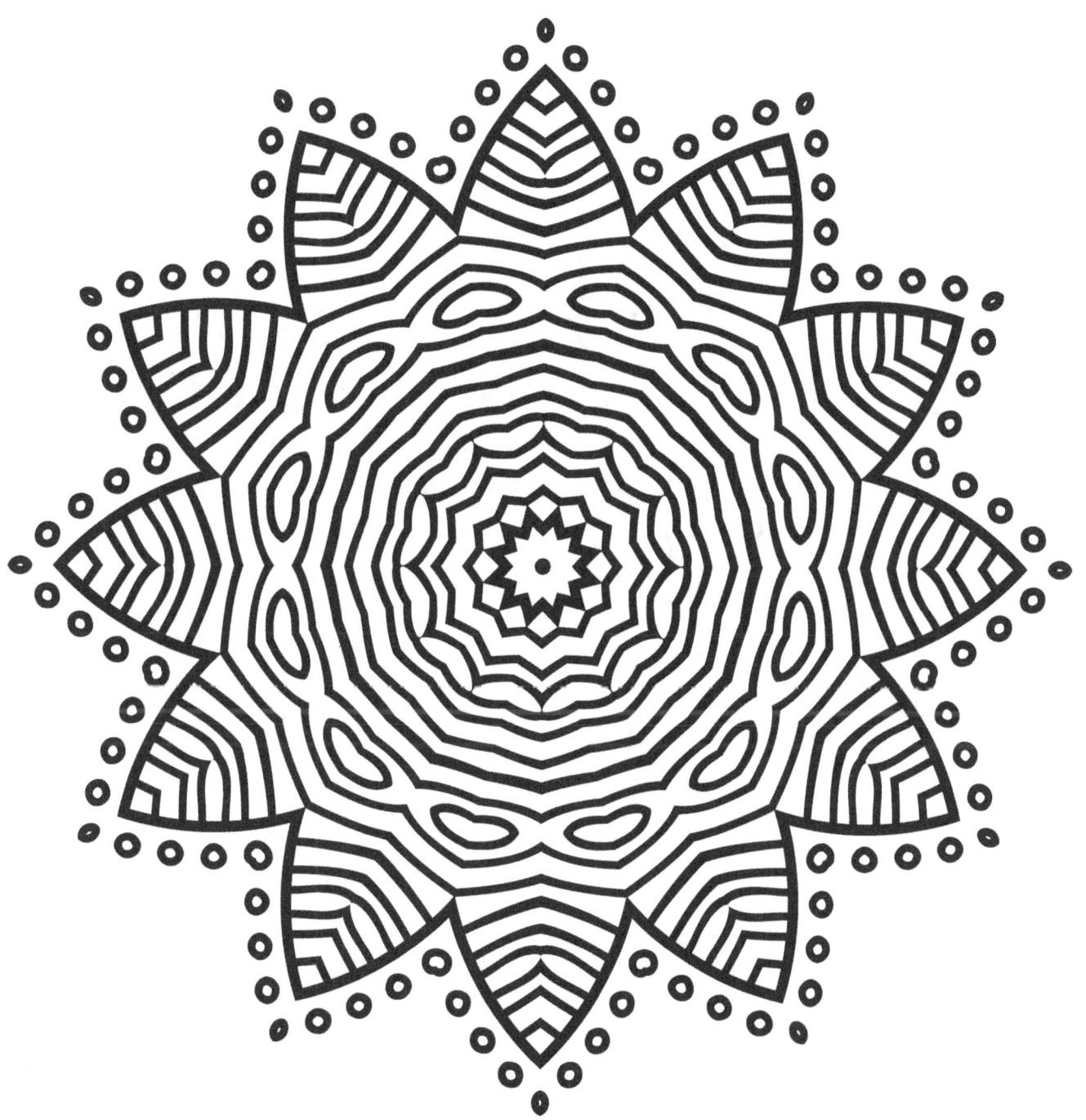

Optimism is the faith that leads to achievement.
Nothing can be done without
hope and confidence.

-Helen Keller

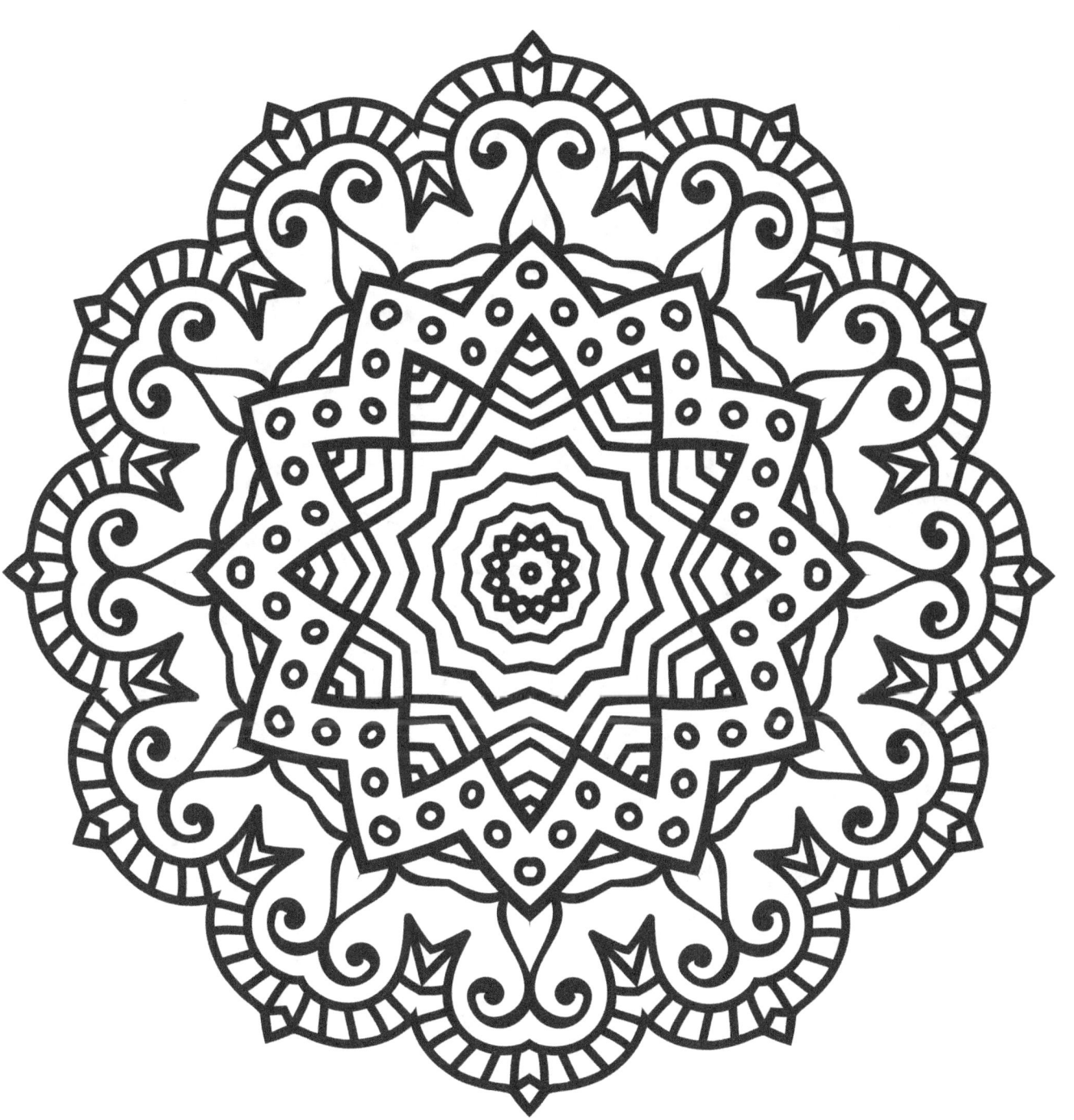

We may encounter many defeats but we must
not be defeated.

-Maya Angelou

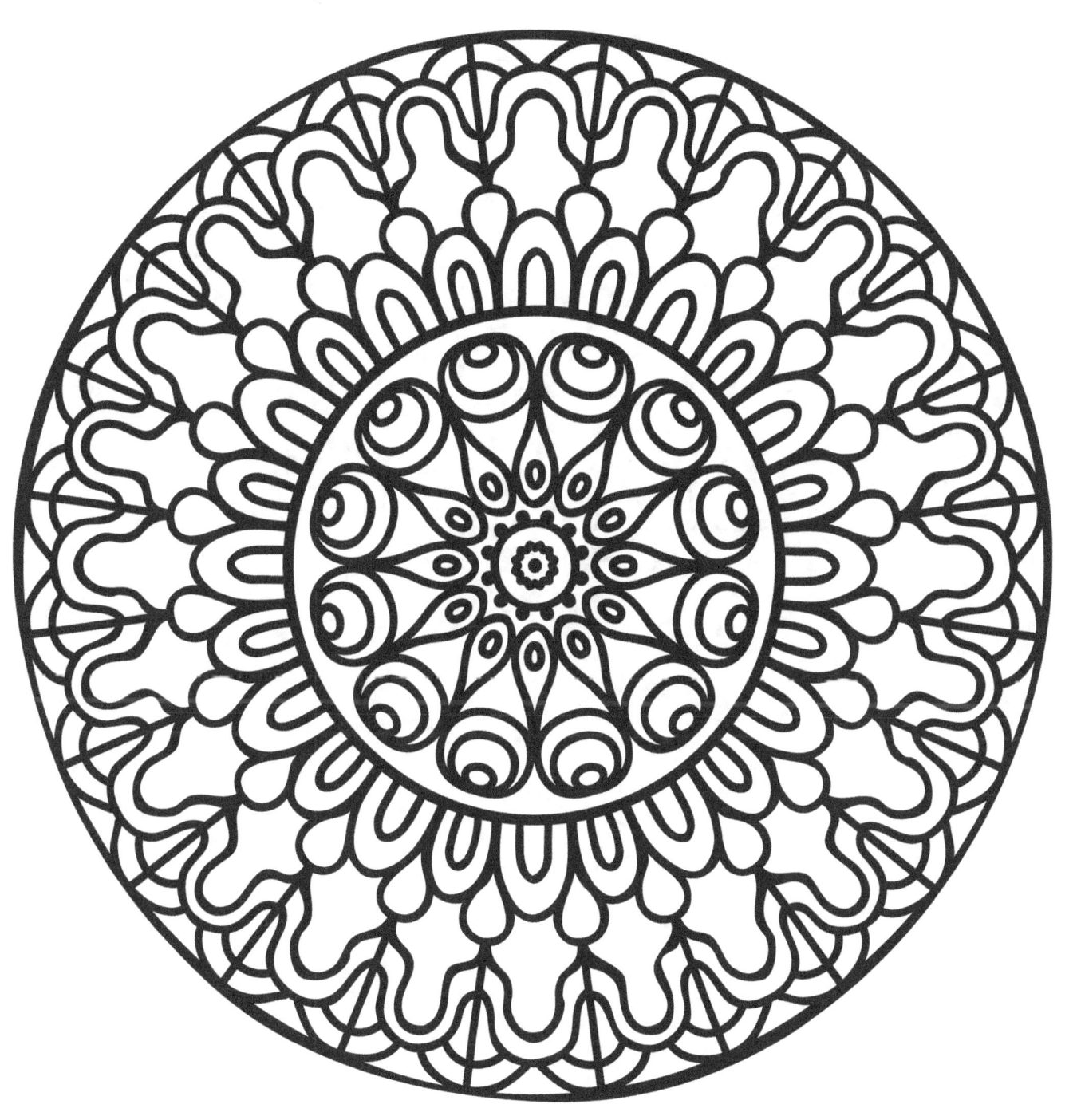

Perseverance is failing 19 times and
succeeding the 20th.

-Julie Andrews

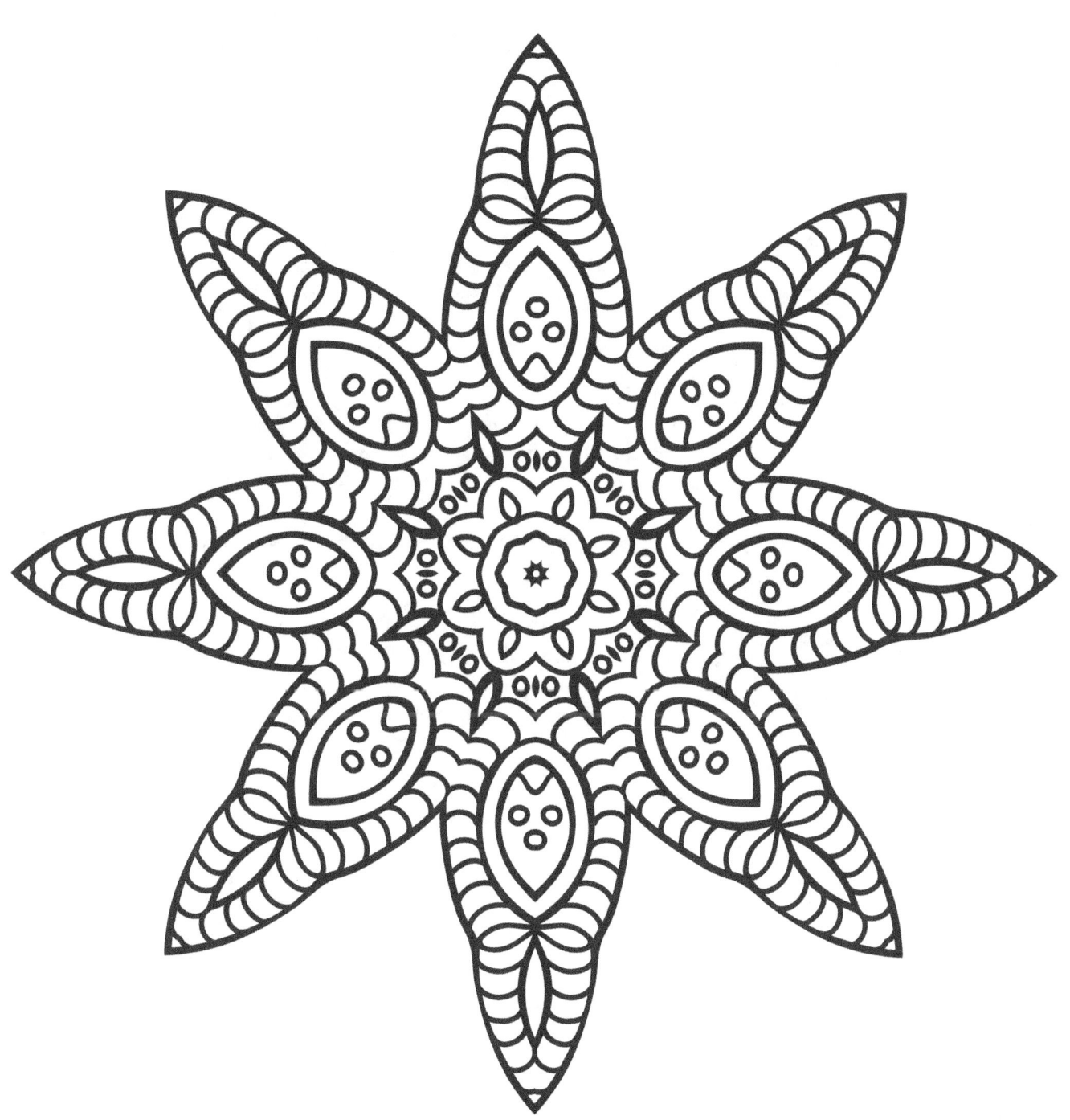

Either I will find a way, or I will make one.

-Philip Sidney

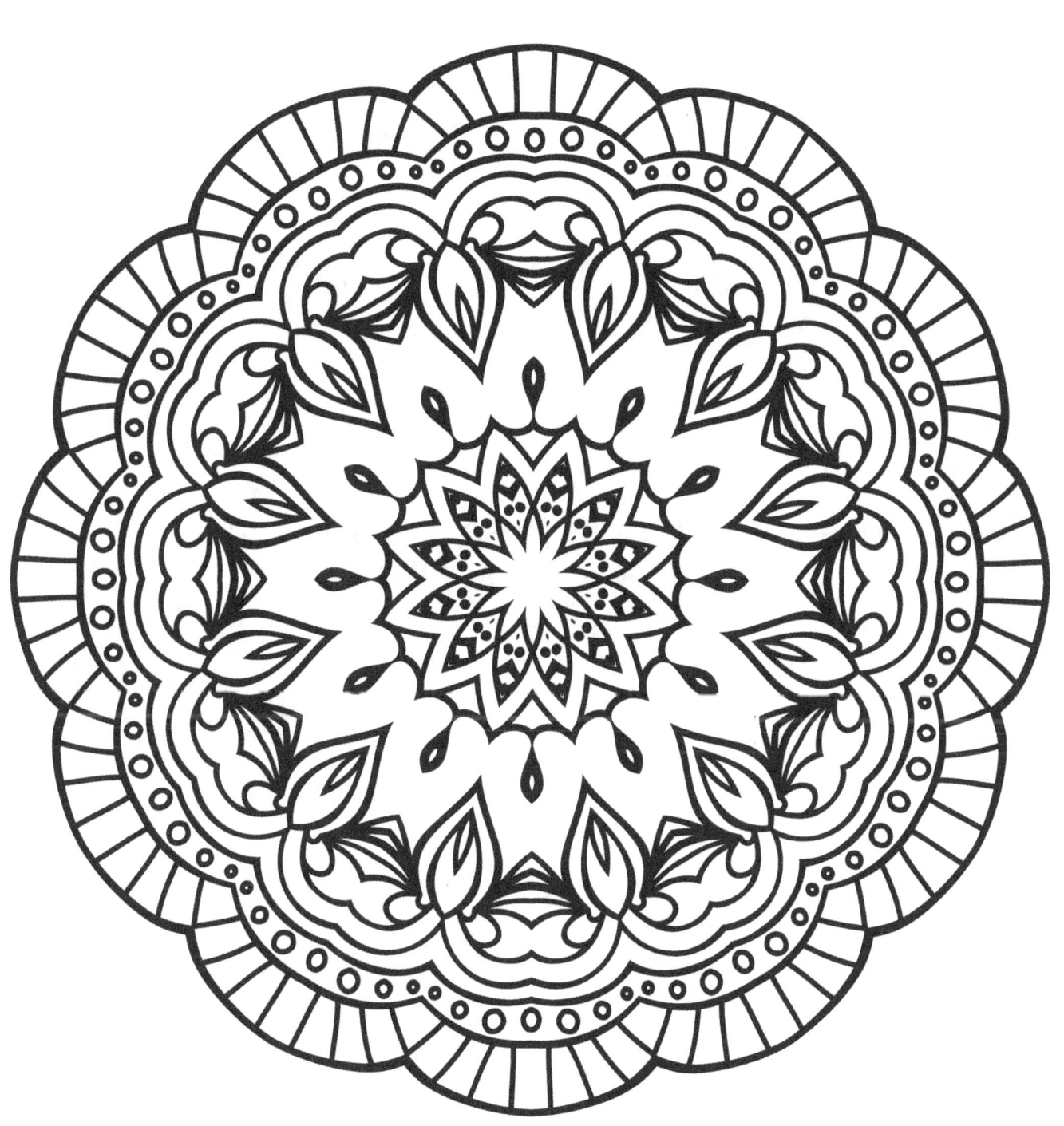

Accept the challenges so that you can feel
the exhilaration of victory.

-George S. Patton

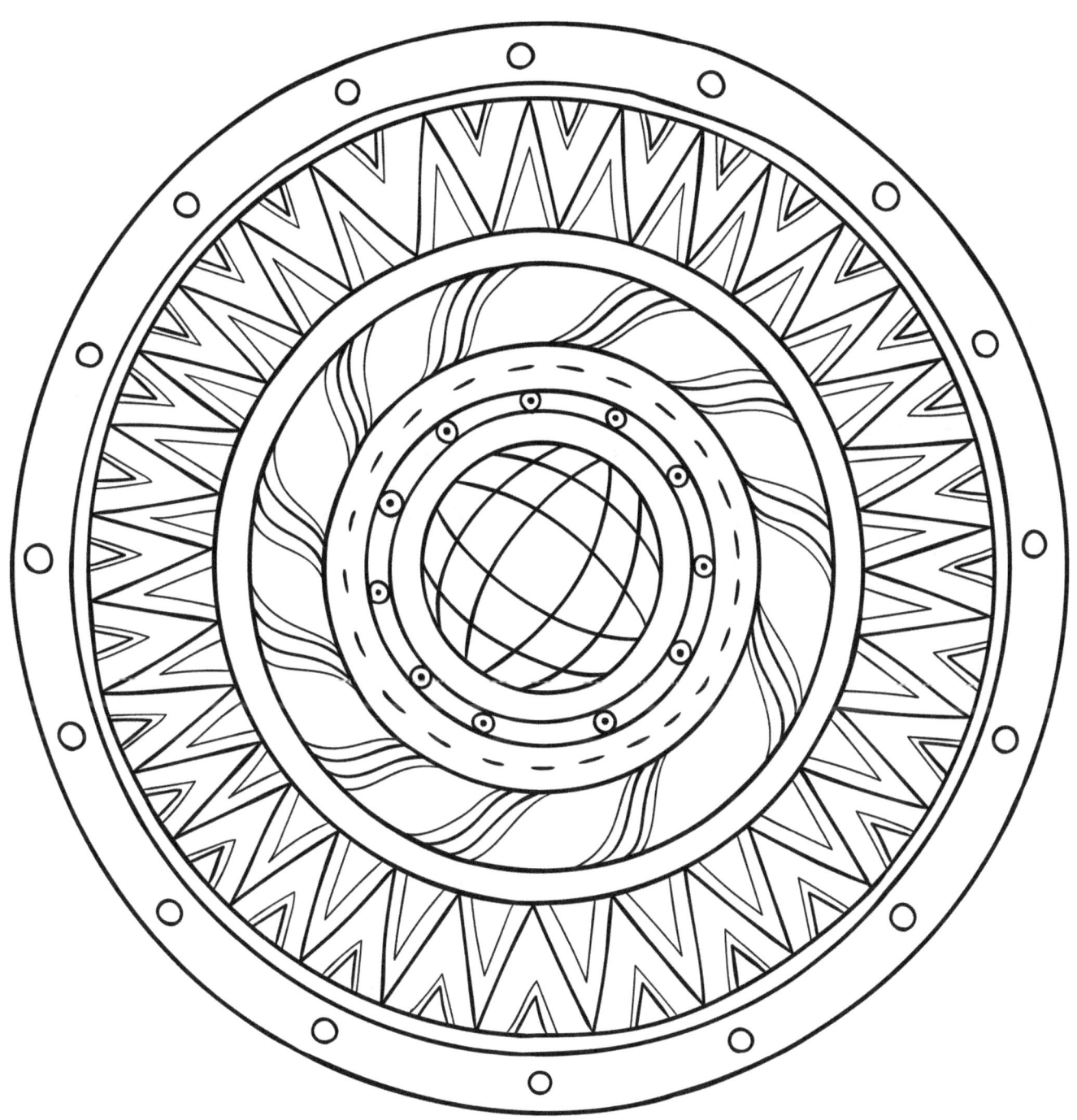

Perseverance is not a long race; it is many
short races one after the other.

-Walter Elliot

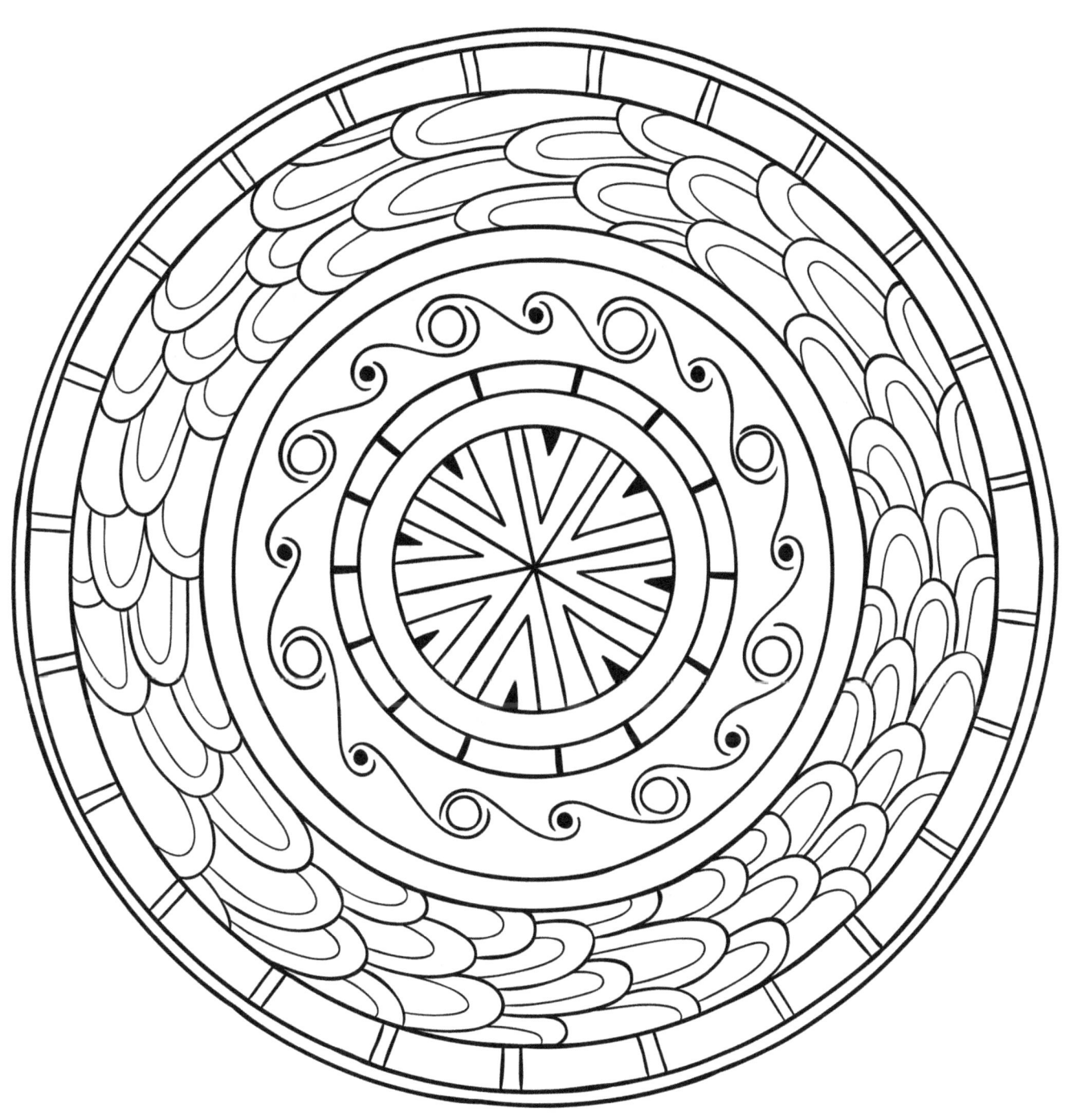

If you fell down yesterday, stand up today.

-H. G. Well

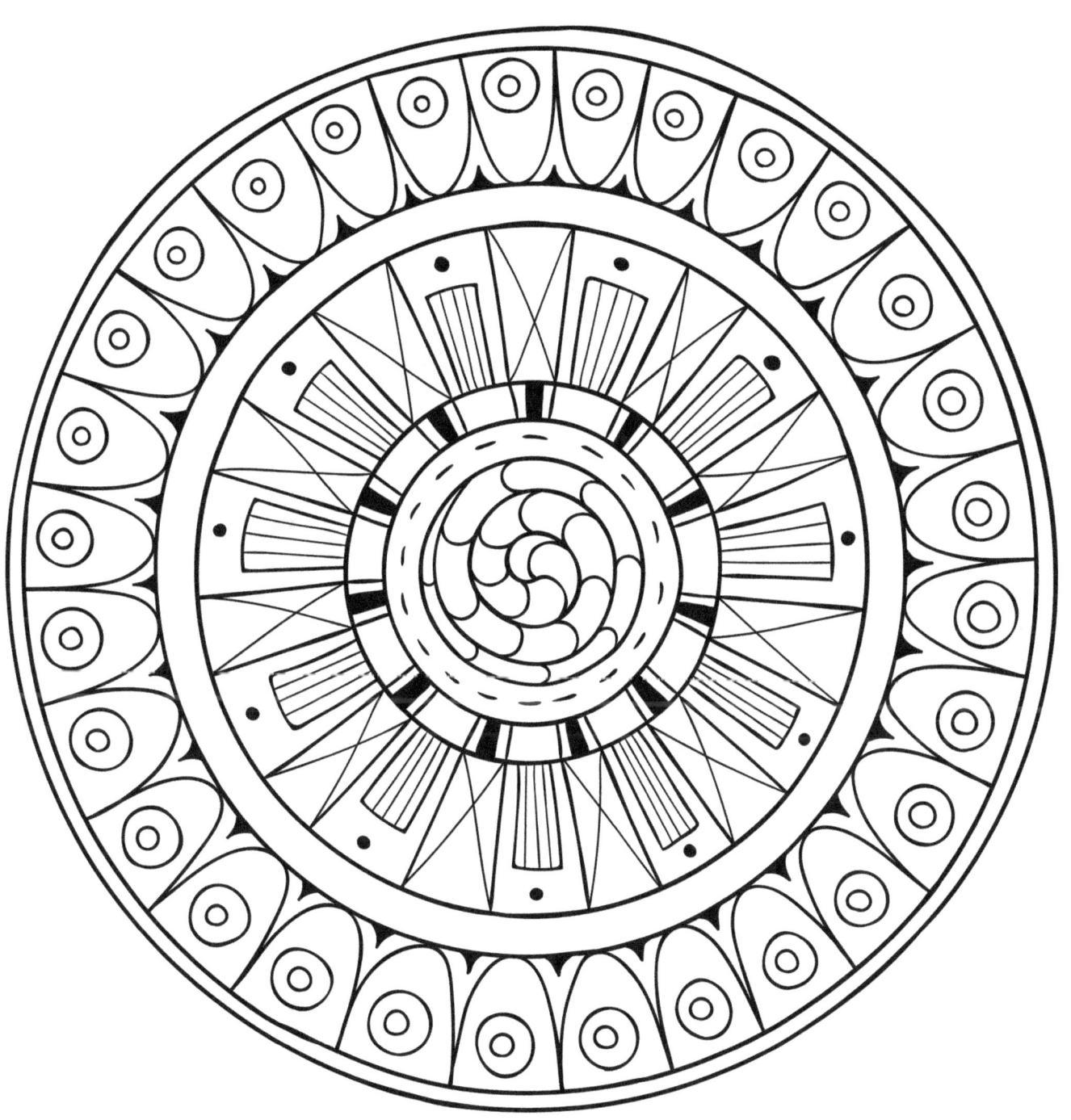

Life is 10% what happens to us and
90% how we react to it.

–Dennis P. Kimbro

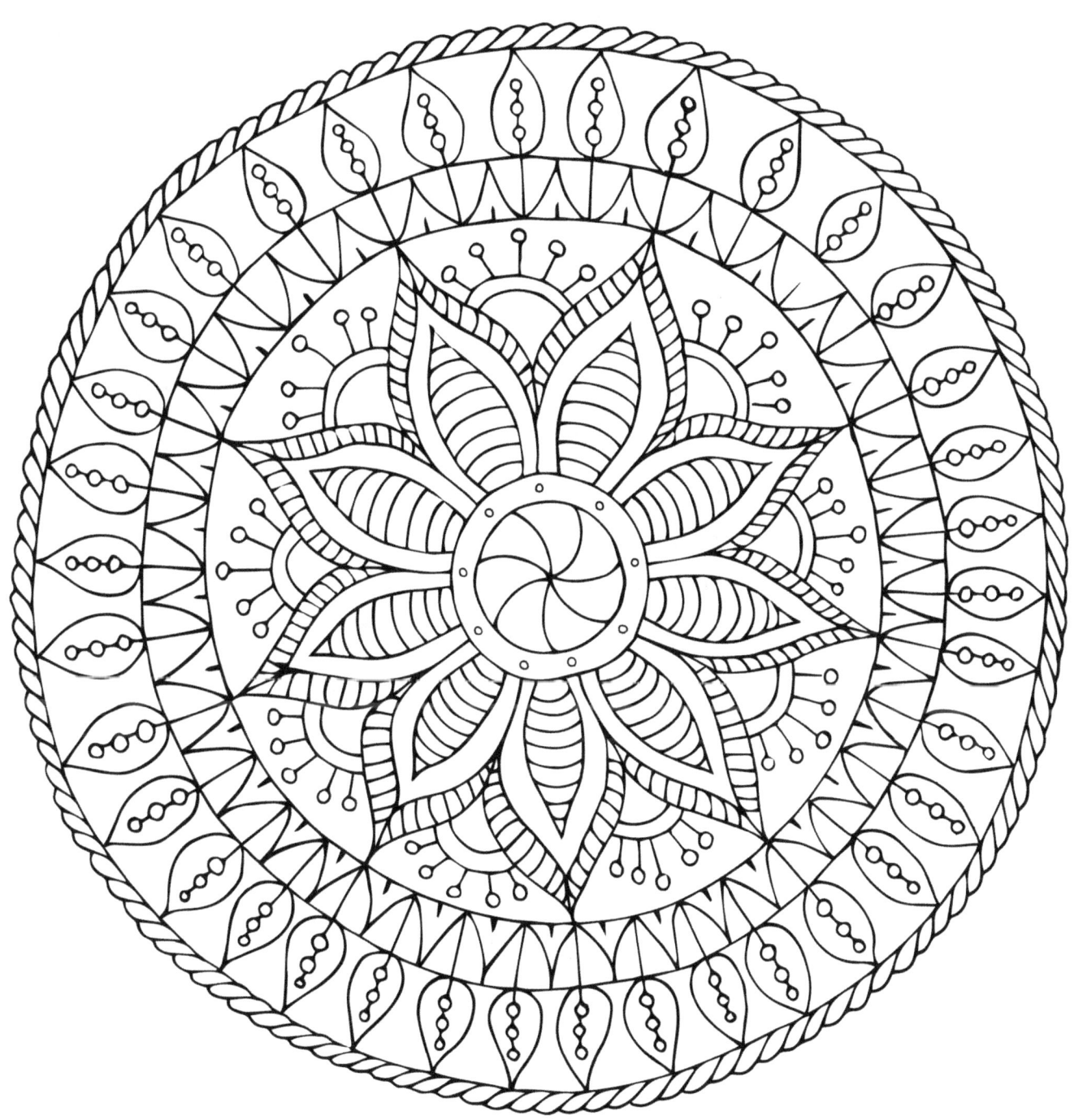

Life has two rules:
1. Never quit.
2. Always remember rule #1.

-Author Unknown

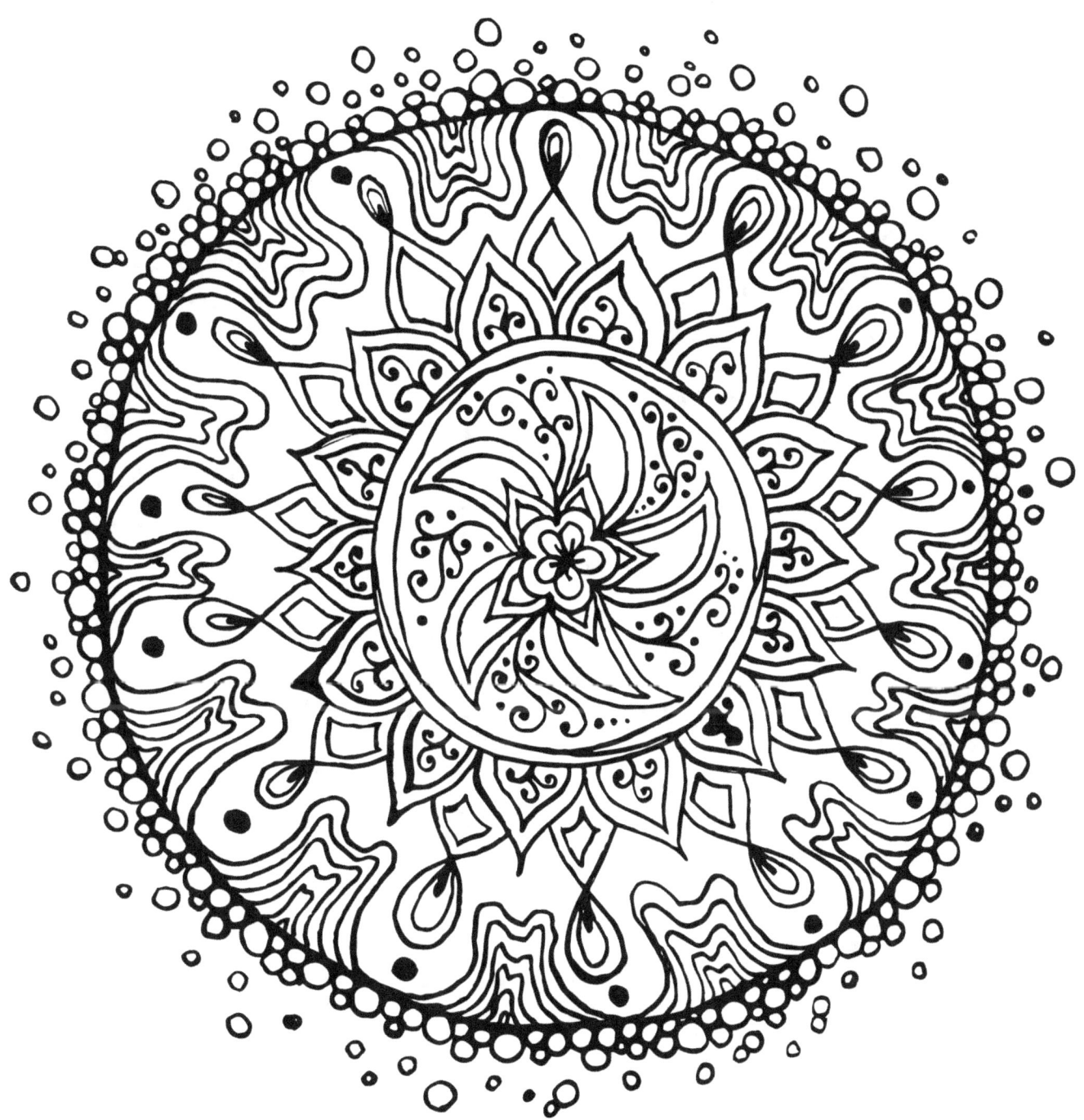

There are two ways of spreading light: to be
the candle or the mirror that reflects it.

-Edith Warton

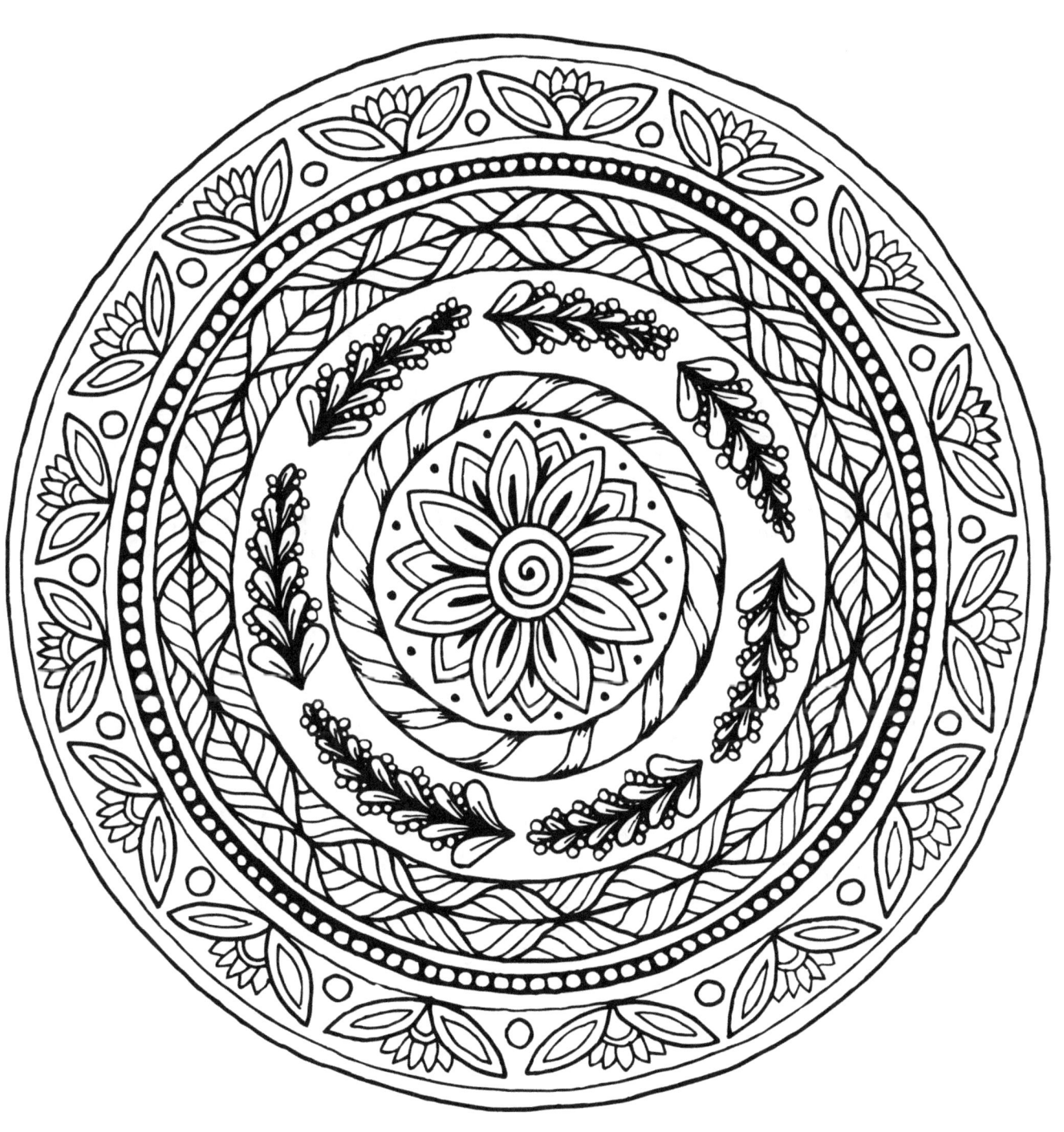

Happiness resides not in possessions, and
not in gold, happiness dwells in the soul.

-Democritus

The real opportunity for success lies within
the person and not in the job.

-Zig Ziglar

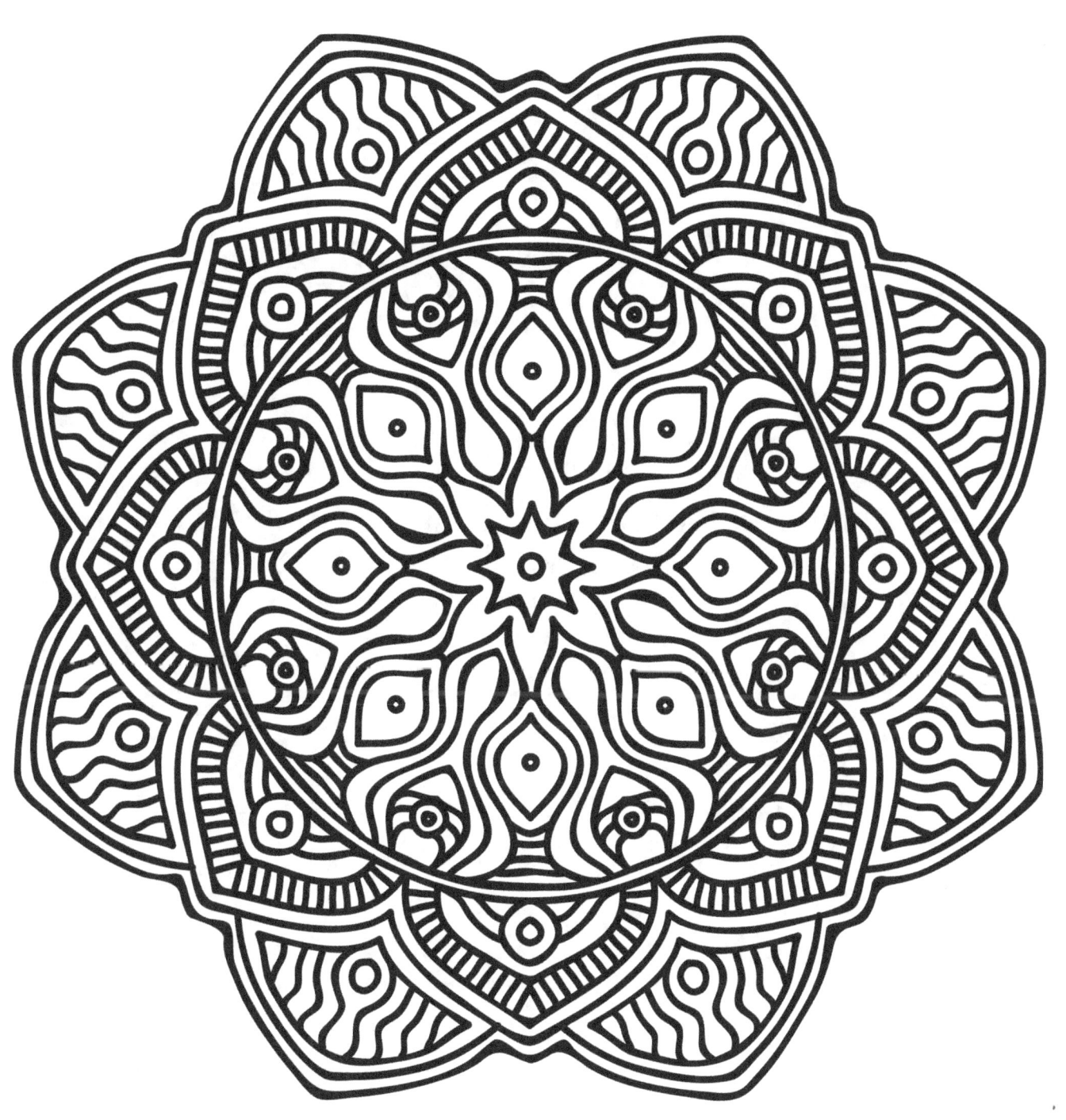

Nurture your mind with great thoughts.
To believe in the heroic makes heroes.

-Benjamin Disraeli

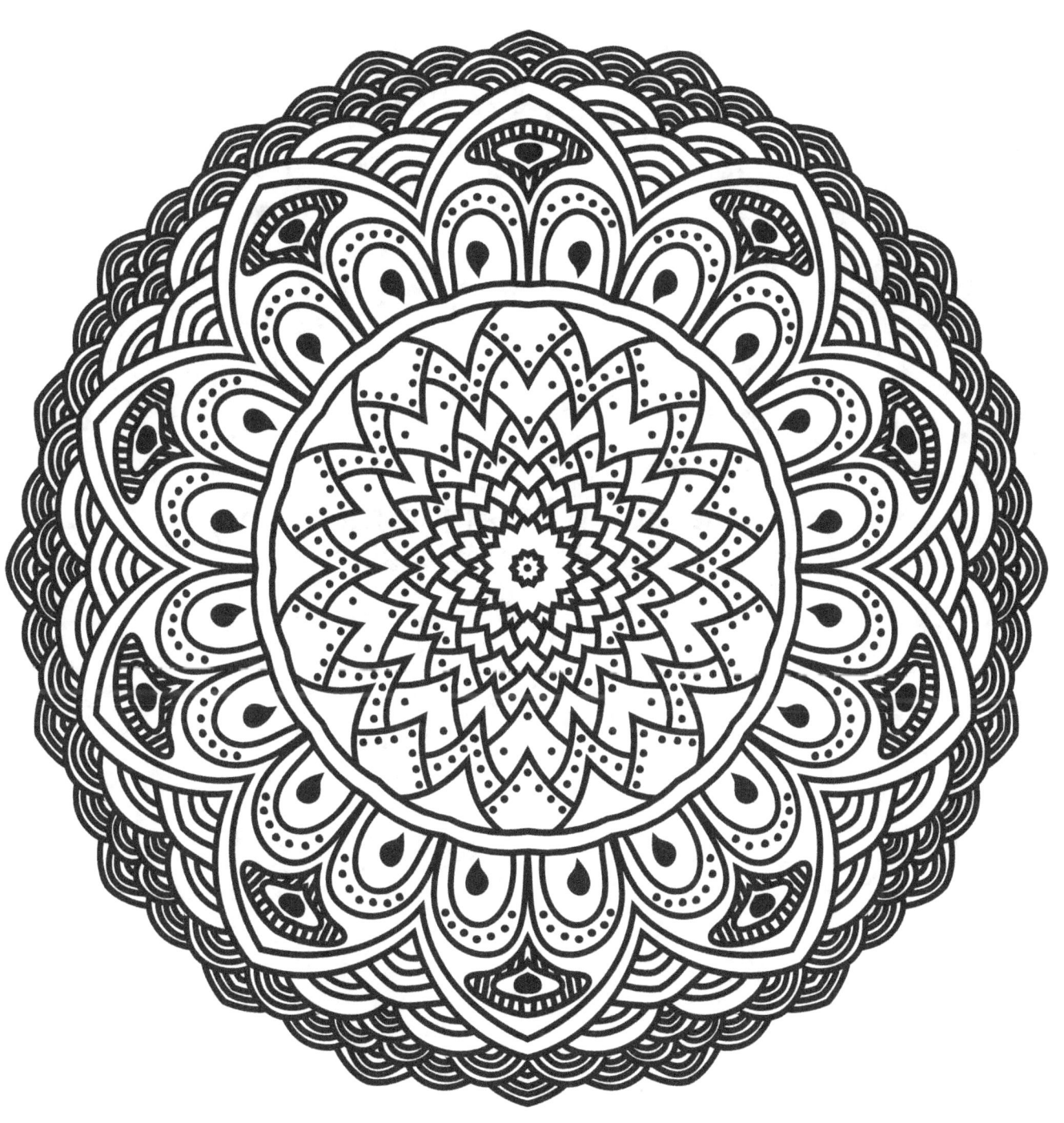

Even if you're on the right track, you'll
get run over if you just sit there.

-Will Rogers

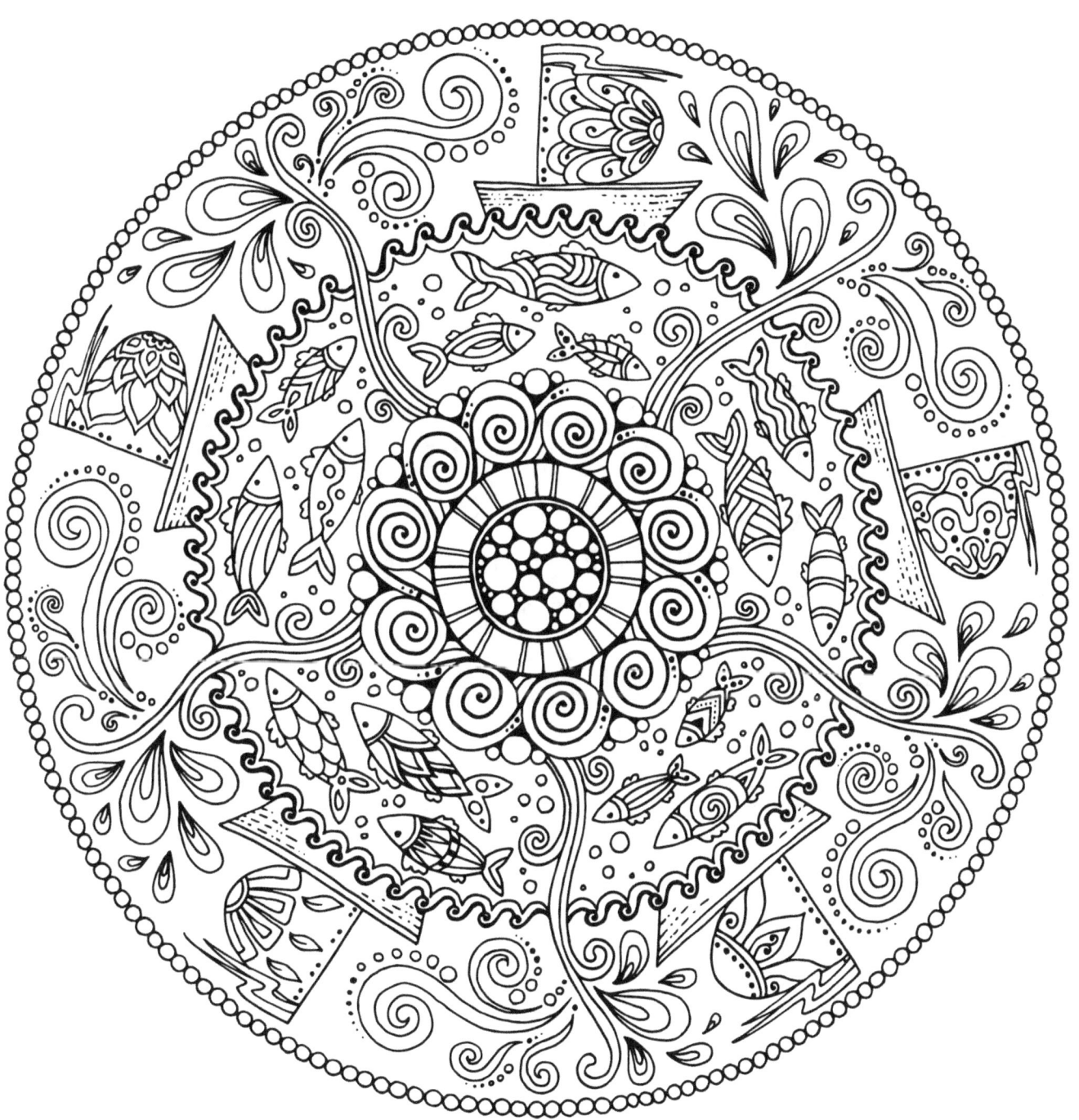

I am thankful for all of those who said NO to me.
It's because of them I'm doing it myself.

-Albert Einstein

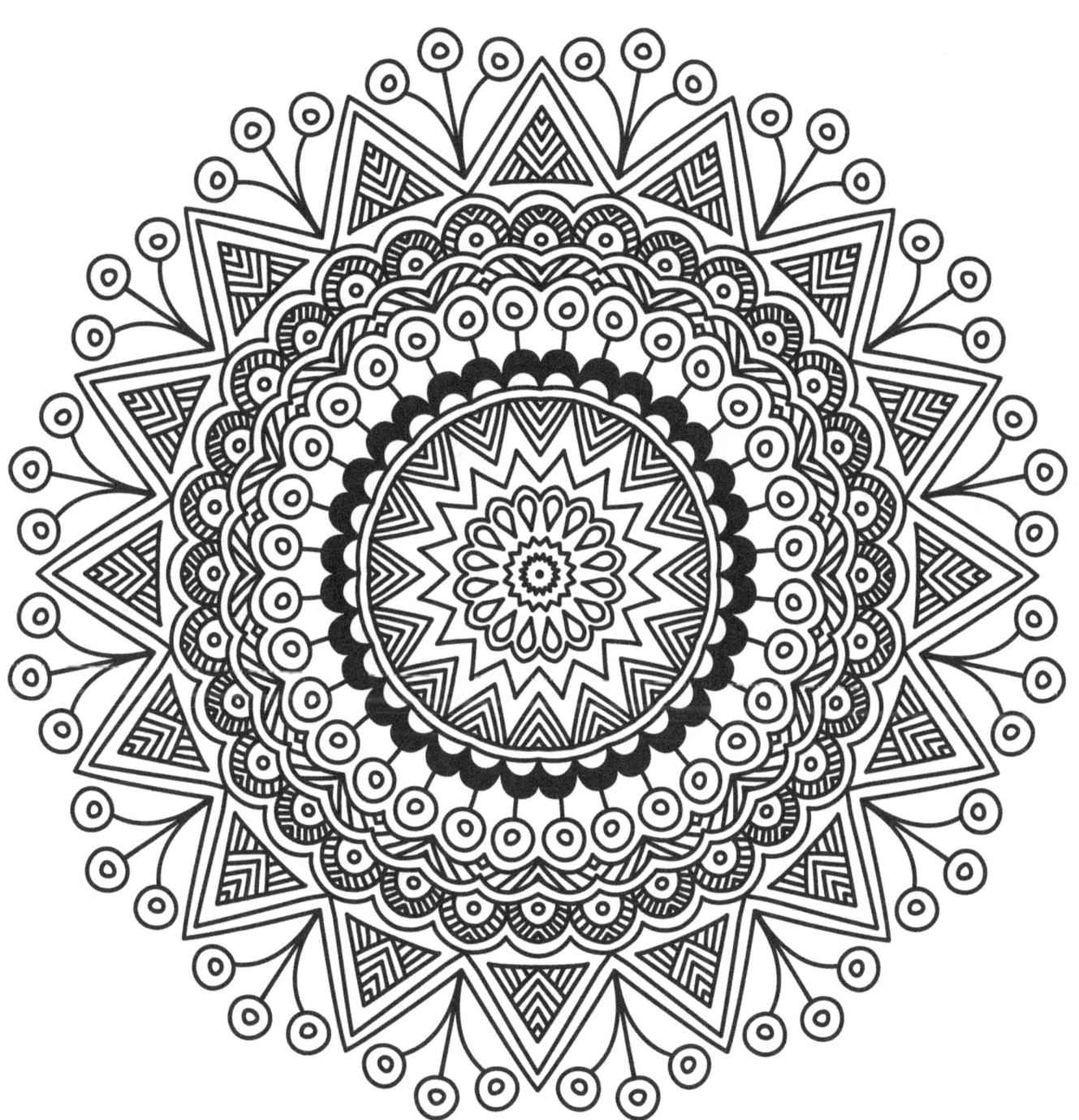